Bonnie & Cory,

Leadership is not what you have,
it's what you give.

Live... Learn... Lead!

RJ Bennett

LEADERSHIP

IS...

(DOT, DOT, DOT)

Bob Bennett

Founder, Achieve-LLC

CLO FedEx Express, Retired

You can have anything you want in life if you just help enough other people get what they want.

Zig Ziglar

Dedication

First and foremost I thank my wife, Gayle, the main person responsible for my transition from engineer to *people person* with an effective blend of left and right brain. I also thank my family, children, and grandchildren, who were the inspiration for many of these lessons. You guys are the best!

A special thanks also goes to my coworkers, especially Ellen Tedford, who patiently helped lead me through my personal transition at work; Sharon Blankenship, who faithfully acted as editor for all the internal blogs that led to this book; Jay Hines who created the packaging for the articles; and the 'GOLDS' team, our department at FedEx Express, for their enthusiastic feedback and urging to share these stories with others.

To those who gave me stories and ideas that help convey these leadership lessons, Walt DeVault, Fr. John Leach, Vera Mullary, Pat Miller, Judy Waters, Ray Murphy, Jorge Veizaga (and any others I have forgotten to mention), thank you!

And I thank all those friends and colleagues, who did not read all the stories but believed enough in the concept to encourage me to make this dream a reality.

Finally, thanks to all who, in any way, contributed to my growth in business and as a person. You helped me learn that we are all leaders in our own way.

Table of Contents

Leadership Is...(Dot, Dot, Dot)

Table of Contents

Leadership Is…(Dot, Dot, Dot)

Forward

I have two 'pet peeves' about perceptions of leadership that I hope to address and dispel in this book. These perceptions are evidenced by a question that is asked often and the response it usually generates:

- "Why are there so few leaders today?"
- "All you have to do to become a (great) leader is…"

I propose that there *are* leaders today. Leadership is displayed every day, in many things we do, but we can't see the forest for the trees. We don't recognize it because today, things change more quickly than ever before, requiring leadership in bites - a reliance on shared and delegated leadership. With no way to predict the circumstances when actions are to be taken, we can't define what leadership competencies will be required and, consequently, don't recognize leadership when it actually occurs.

I believe there are at least six basic false impressions about leaders and leadership that generate the above question and answer. These misconceptions might be clarified if we understand that:

- Leadership is not about your title, positional authority, the number of people who report to you or where you sit in the organization. This stems from what people think a leader does. *A leader makes a difference in someone else's life.* As such, Generals and CEOs can be considered leaders, but so are teachers, firemen, police officers, and aides. When we recognize our parents, siblings, friends, yes, even our children as leaders, we then begin to understand the true meaning of leadership.

- <u>A leader is not a person who does something</u>, but rather is someone who inspires others to achieve greater heights. A leader recognizes that the only person who can make a change in your life is you, and then provides the environment and the encouragement for you to take action. Leadership is not the result, it is the behavior and actions one takes.
- <u>Leadership is not about budgets</u>, programs implemented, the wealth you have or the records you break. Leadership comes from inside; it is all about you – your ability and desire to recognize, respond to and overcome the challenges that you face every day of your life. Heroes are not those individuals who have no fear; they are the ones that act in spite of their fear. The same can be said of leaders.
- <u>Leadership is highly complex</u>; there is no 'silver bullet' or 'best practices' or even a set of competencies or behaviors that one can follow to earn the title of leader. There is no checklist to follow to become a great leader. It is situation dependent. The skills that make you a great leader in one setting may be irrelevant, or even detrimental, in another.
- <u>There is no light switch</u>, no event, no bit of knowledge that turns someone into a leader. It is in the application of the knowledge you possess, the values that you hold, and the person that you are, that make you a leader. While we all may be born with leadership capabilities, these aptitudes must be recognized and developed to make them effective. The answer to the question, Are leaders born or made? is yes!
- <u>The title of leader is transient</u>. It is the accumulation of behaviors and actions that makes a person a true or great leader. One improper behavior, even just the *perception* of impropriety, can destroy all the good you

have accomplished. Leaders earn their title every minute of every day.

There have been many books written on leadership professing to have the answer. But leadership can't be clearly defined. It is not one, two, or even three dimensional. Leadership is demonstrated through a myriad of actions inspired by skills and competencies - most of which we already possess. This book is an attempt to demystify leadership and make you aware of a seventh truth about leadership:

- <u>You, too, have leadership traits</u> and are a leader just by virtue of who you are!

It is my hope that this book, these stories, provide you with a renewed and broader perspective of leadership and generate some thought as to the definition of a leader – the definition of you!

Culture

[**kuhl**-cher]:

...the shared attitudes, values, practices, beliefs, customs, arts, way of thinking and behaviors that exist in a place or organization (such as a business) at a particular time

Synonym: accomplishment
Antonyms: barbarianism, savage

Leadership Is...

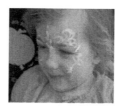

Culture

Don't you just love grandkids!? I am blessed to have five. I feel blessed, but not because they are so much fun, they keep me young, you can spoil them all you want, or you can return them when you have had enough. No, I am blessed because they teach me something new every day, things about love, life and, yes, even leadership and business.

My wife and I took two of our grandchildren, May and Tucker, to Disney World for vacation. Allow me to provide a little background. First, they are twins. May is 3 minutes older than her brother, which may partially explain why she manipulator, gleefully starting the count-down, '1,2...,' while Tucker is poised to 'surf' down the stairs on a rug, jump off the playhouse roof, or do any number of things no one over the age of 30 would ever consider sane. Second, at the time of this trip, they were one week shy of their third birthday. They most definitely were full of energy. And third, they are like the children who live in Lake Woebegone. For those of you not familiar with this community, their children are all above average.

Now, to unleash these children on unsuspecting guests, even at a Disney hotel, just didn't seem fair so we stayed at a cabin in the Wilderness Village. We spent four days at 4 separate theme parks, sometimes going to more than one park a day. They kids were troopers, often not going to bed until midnight, thanks in part to their legs not working between rides which required us to carry them. This made for some pretty long days but allowed them to go on every ride that did not have a height restriction at least once.

While packing to leave after the adventure, my wife and I debated over what we thought were the kids' favorite rides. After much thought and discussion, the decision was: Tucker – Toy Story; May – Ariel. So, like many intelligent, confident grown-ups, we had to confirm our brilliance by asking them.

The first surprise for us was the speed with which they answered the question, "What was your favorite ride?" Surely there were so many that they would need a minute to think about it, but no. They both answered immediately: Tucker shouted first, "The Magic Stairs," followed by May's scream of "The School bus!"

After a few minutes, we realized the Magic Stairs were, in fact, the escalator that led up to the Land ride. And the school bus? It was the shuttle that took us between the cabin and the theme parks.

- Do we ever assume we know what people are thinking?

These answers were not what we expected, so we pressed a little further and asked them, "What was your next favorite ride?" Again, without any hesitation, they answered: "The playground" from May, and "The Magic bed" from Tucker, who must have known we were at the Magic Kingdom. The playground was right next to the cabin and was identical to the one we go to in our home town. The Magic bed was the Murphy bed in the cabin – magic because he could make it appear and disappear at whim! This answer appeared to be a little strange because we have a Murphy bed in our condo, where we stay with them often and on which Tucker sleeps when he is there.

After some thought, we understood their answers: the Magic Stairs was a new adventure that was scary to a 3 year old, but by riding it he accomplished something he did not know was possible; and he did it while holding our hand, safe in the knowledge we were there for him. The School bus was where we sang songs and talked about all the fun we had together so far during the trip – and it also provided the anticipation/vision of what was to come, creating excitement for the day's outings. The playground was the place we interacted, helped each other swing, come down the slide, and just be together and enjoy the time. The Magic bed was not only something out of the ordinary, it was a place of comfort as well; we sat and slept on it – together.

- Are we always looking for the 'big' idea to impress and endear our employees?

- Do we recognize the importance of what we do and how we make people feel rather than the provision of a tangible gift?

- Can we look at things through the eyes of a child, with appreciation?

We did give it one last try – even though we should have known better. "What was your next favorite?" was answered the same by both – The cabin! That should not have been a surprise either; it was a place where we stayed, where we were with family, and that was associated with pleasant things. The cabin - it was **our** place – somewhere that we shared and treasured and a safe port in a storm of new and exciting adventures

Our work environment, our culture, is the cabin in which we all exist. We have all experienced it – the purchase and presentation of an expensive, large toy for our children and grandchildren that, when unwrapped, sits idle while they play with the box it came in. Perhaps as leaders we need to spend time working on the 'box' we give our employees, remembering it is the little things we do daily for our family that make up our culture, our box.

Culture

The importance of culture

- "(Culture is)...a system of collectively held values" ~ *Geert Hofstede*
- "(Culture is)...basic assumptions and beliefs shared by members of an organization" - *Edgar Schein*
- "...culture is everything." - *Louis V. Gerstner, Jr. former CEO IBM*
- "... firms with cultures that emphasized all the key managerial constituencies (customers, stockholders, and employees) and leadership from managers at all levels outperformed firms that did not have those cultural traits by a huge margin." - *John Kotter & James Heskett, Harvard Business School, Corporate Culture and Performance*

Ways leaders establish a positive culture

- Educate and train employees
- Be open and receptive – hold employee forums
- Ask for participation - in meetings as well as strategic and tactical planning
- Use policy as a *guideline* in handling individual circumstances
- Explain in detail the direction and purpose of efforts
- Learn the names of employees (and their family members)
- Look for and take advantage of opportunities to say 'thank you'
- Be visible, walk around and visit employees at their job
- Listen and care
- 'Roll up your sleeves'; work side-by-side with employees
- Look for and celebrate the 'little things'

Problem Solving
[**prob**-l*uh* m **solv-ng**]:

...to find a way to deal with and end something that is difficult to deal with, something that is a source of trouble, worry, etc.

Synonyms: answer, work out
Antonyms: leave unknown, keep hanging

Leadership is...

Problem Solving

We are all good at something. We may have a natural ability or we may learn it over time. For example, I am pretty good with laundry now. This ability is a result of my wife's patience during times of trial and error, which included wearing pink underwear for a few weeks.

One aspect of laundry I still struggle with, however, is the folding of certain pieces of clothing. I can't tell if they are inside out or not; there are too many strings and not enough substance—those of you with teen-age girls know this well. Sometimes things get so tangled there is no hope of straightening them out! But this story is not about me, it is about my youngest child, Cameron.

Being good parents, my wife and I wanted to ensure our children had all the opportunities that we didn't have growing up. So when my daughter was old enough to begin dance lessons we enrolled her in ballet and tap classes.

During one lesson, shortly after getting dressed, she calmly stated she had to go to the restroom. Being from the north, I thought this phenomena only occurred bundling your children up for the winter snow; little did I know it was also true for ballet! Cameron resolutely marched off to the restroom, emphatically telling us she could 'do it myself! ' But we knew the challenge for a four year old of taking off and putting back on a leotard could prove to be overwhelming. As expected, the leotard, after removal, was inside out and hopelessly twisted. She could not get it back on, no matter how hard she tried.

I am sure you can imagine the various reactions a 3 year old may have in this situation. She might sit there and cry about her fate; she might continue to struggle with the garment knowing that it was a losing battle; she might have waited patiently for mom, who would eventually wonder where she was and come to help. But Cameron didn't do any of those things.

She came out of the bathroom, stark naked, except for the ballet slippers she still had on her feet. She was holding her twisted leotard in one hand and had an exasperated but determined look on her face. She ignored everyone else in the studio, marched straight over to the instructor and, with one hand on her hip and the other waving the leotard, she asked the teacher to help.

- Do we have the courage to take on challenges?

- Do we give up when challenges are too great?

- Are we afraid, as leaders, to 'bare ourselves' to others and admit we don't have all the answers?

My daughter wasn't ashamed; she was determined! She solved her problem using the resources available to her, with the only lasting consequence being the admiration and pride of those who witnessed this act of bravery!

Problem Solving

Thoughts on problem solving

- "How you think about a problem is more important than the problem itself, so always think positively." – *Norman Vincent Peale*
- "It is so much easier to suggest solutions when you don't know much about the problem." – *Malcolm S. Forbes*
- "(Ask yourself,) what other explanation can there be?" – *Hercule Poirot, Agatha Christie, Murder on the Orient Express*
- "Leaders must have the courage to battle when necessary, but perhaps more importantly, the wisdom to know which battles to fight." – *Bob Bennett*

Ways leaders problem solve

- Start with the end in mind, a clear definition of requirements and expectations
- Rely on facts and data rather than intuition and emotion; use proven quality practices
- Establish a diverse team of subject matter experts, improvement experts, customers, and users
- Be open; listen to and seriously consider ideas from all sources; there is no hierarchy in problem solving
- Ask for help
- Choose good (bottom-line) metrics
- Prepare an implementation plan and team
- Hold Business Review meetings regularly with officer and stakeholders to ensure buy-in
- Conduct After Action Reviews to improve future opportunities

Humility

[hyoo-**mil**-i-tee *or, often,* yoo-]:

...the quality or condition of being <u>humble</u> and/or having a modest opinion or estimate of one's own importance, rank, etc.

Synonyms: humbleness, modesty
Antonyms: pride, arrogance, conceit

Leadership Is...

Humility

In college, I had a fraternity brother who was born and raised in a cattle area of Texas. We became close, so I invited him to visit my home on Long Island. While there, we took a side trip into New York City where he was amazed at the rudeness of the cab drivers, citing their language and gestures.

The next year, he invited me to visit him on his family's ranch. Referencing the cabbies, which obviously had a lasting impression on him, he told me the people here would be much different from what I was accustomed. When asked how so, he told me this story, supposedly about one of his neighbors, if you can call someone 20 miles away a neighbor. I am not sure if it's true since I recently saw it on the internet, but it's an excellent lesson in leadership. It went something like this:

A DEA officer stopped at a ranch in Texas to talk to an old rancher. He told the rancher, "I need to inspect your ranch for illegal drugs." The rancher was cooperative, friendly and ready to help. "Okay, but don't go in that field over there," he said, pointing to a location past the tree line.

The DEA officer verbally exploded and said, "Mister, I have the authority of the federal government with me." Reaching into his back pants pocket, he removed his badge and proudly displayed it to the rancher. "See this badge? This badge means I am allowed to go wherever I wish... on any land! No questions asked; no answers given! Have I made myself clear? Do you understand?"

The rancher nodded politely, apologized and went back to work.

A short time later, the old rancher heard a loud scream and saw the DEA officer running for his life across the field. He was being chased by the rancher's big Santa Gertrudis bull. With every step the bull was gaining ground on the officer, and it seemed likely he would be gored before he could reach safety. The officer was clearly terrified. The rancher threw down his tools, ran to the fence and yelled at the top of his lungs...

"Your badge, show him your badge!"

- Are we so enamored with our own position and power that we use it to *get* our way rather than to *find* our way?
- Do we ignore the sound advice from our employees and peers?
- Do we encourage employees to participate and innovate or to watch and wait?

Humility

Thoughts on humility

- "The fullest and best ears of corn hang lowest toward the ground." - *Bishop Reynold*
- "It is unwise to be too sure of one's own wisdom. It is healthy to be reminded that the strongest might weaken and the wisest might err." - *Mahatma Gandhi*
- "Leaders are not intimidators. They are motivators who listen to and learn from their employees, peers and customers." – *Bob Bennett*

Ways leaders show humility

- Speak as little as possible about yourself; use 'you' or 'we', not 'I'
- Don't impose your process/way on others; recognize there are and allow alternate ways to get to the desired result
- Allow mistakes
- Request input, thoughts and ideas
- Accept and respond through actions to feedback, good and bad
- Allow others to present results
- Give credit to others
- Avoid using positional power to get things done; influence and inspire
- Delegate major projects; trust employees to get it done

Ethics

[**eth**-ik z]:

...the moral principles or values that are deemed important which govern the conduct and behaviors of a culture, individual or a group

Synonyms: moral, value
Antonym: immoral, unprincipled

Leadership Is...

Ethics

On December 20, 1943, B-17 bomber pilot Charles Brown, then 21, flying his first combat mission, looked out his cockpit window and saw a German fighter flying just off his wing. The B-17 was badly damaged. Its tail gunner had been killed; other crew members were injured and the skin on the plane was shredded. They were an easy target.

Just minutes before, a German ace fighter pilot, Franz Stigler, was on the tarmac when he saw a crippled American B-17 bomber flying incredibly low over his German airfield. He rushed to his plane and with a crisp salute he took off in pursuit of the obviously lost and troubled American plane. Sigler was one kill away from winning Germany's highest award for valor, the Knight's Cross. This was his chance for eternal fame and recognition! And if that was not enough of a reason to jump to action, Stigler had yet another reason, one much more personal. Earlier in the war, Stigler's brother had been killed in an American raid.

As Stigler approached the bomber, he expected resistance but found none. He could see the blood soaked tail gunner slumped over his gun. He could see through the shredded fuselage to the crew members tending to one another's severe injuries. Yes, they were an easy target - too easy.

Stigler moved his fighter in position to see the cockpit of the B-17 and there was Charles Brown and his co-pilot, Spencer Luke, frantically trying to keep the large aircraft air born. Their eyes met and Stigler could see the fear and panic in Brown and Luke's eyes.

As he retold the story, Stigler recalled the words of his commanding officer, "You follow the rules of war for you, not for your enemy." It was at that moment that Stigler removed his finger from the trigger.

Rather than taking the easy kill, Stigler moved his plane below the already low flying American plane, putting himself in position so that the German anti-aircraft guns on the ground would not fire on the two planes. Flying in this position for miles, Stigler escorted the bomber to the North Sea where the threat of German attack was no longer a concern. The B-17, even though now over friendly airspace, was so badly damaged that its chance of returning to England safely was far from certain. Stigler, as he turned to return to base, knew he had done all he could to save the Americans. The plane's fate and that of its crew was now out of his hands.

Despite all odds, Brown was able to land the crippled B-17 safely at a base in England. Both Brown and Stigler returned to their lives, each not knowing the fate of the other.

Charles Brown, however, thought often of the anonymous German pilot and his noble and intrepid actions that day, and after searching for him for some time, eventually found him. While Charles lived the "American dream," Franz was virtually exiled from Germany. He lost his brother, his friends and his fellow pilots - of the 28,000 German pilots, he was one of only 1,000 who survived.

Charles and Franz became close friends, meeting and vacationing together frequently. But it was at a special reunion of that B-17 crew to which Franz was invited, where Charles showed pictures of the family members - the children and grandchildren - those that were alive only because of the decision made by Franz years ago in a far-away land, that the true impact of the decision on that fateful day was finally revealed: Three generations of individuals, all contributing to and enjoying life because of one man's willingness to think of others before himself and do the right thing.

- Do we put ourselves above others?

- Do we pursue our goals and quest for fame without consideration of its impact on others?

- Do we stop to consider the long term impact of our decisions?

- Do we do what is expected, or what is right?

Having allies, friends, and partners is far more valuable than eliminating our competition, receiving transient rewards or even getting revenge.

Ethics

Thoughts on ethics

- "Being good is good business." - *Dame Anita Roddick*
- "The (leader) exists to make sensible exceptions to general rules." – *Elting E. Morison, Professor*
- "We do not act rightly because we have virtue or excellence, but rather we have those because we have acted rightly." – *Aristotle*
- "Nearly all men can withstand adversity, but if you want to test a man's character, give him power." – *Abraham Lincoln.*
- "Law is about what is legal and illegal but ethics are about what is right and wrong." – *Bob Bennett*

Ways leaders display ethics

- Align your values with those of the organization
- Be consistent in your behaviors
- "Walk the talk," do what you say and exhibit the behavior you expect of others
- Use policies as guidelines; treat each issue on its own circumstances
- Clearly define expectations
- Respect the values of others; treat everyone with respect
- Review values (with others) periodically and adapt, as necessary to changing times
- Be fair and consistent in performance evaluations and career opportunities
- Do what is right, not necessarily what is expected
- Give credit where credit is due

Customer Fanatic

[**kuhs**-t*uh*-mer f*uh*-**nat**-ik]:

...a person with an extreme and uncritical enthusiasm or zeal for someone that purchases or uses a commodity, good or service or a person with whom one has dealings

Synonyms: enthusiast, zealot
Antonyms: middle-of-the road, uncaring

Leadership Is...

Being a Customer Fanatic

After my junior year in high school, this 16 year old decided it was time to earn a little spending money, so I took my first summer job. Being something of a geek at the time - *I know, for those of you who know me that's pretty hard to believe* - I procured a job in a cemetery. The position suited me well. It didn't require me to talk with anyone. I could work independently, at my own pace, and I was outside. What else could a teenage future engineer ask for at that age?

- Do we recognize the value of working to live rather than living to work - the importance of doing something you love?

At the beginning of my second week on the job, the manager of the cemetery came out and talked with his only 3 employees, Tom an 80+ year old with a missing finger from an accident that occurred sometime over the 70 years he worked there, Greg a thirty-something individual who, as you would imagine, did most of the heavy lifting, and me.

A widow of one of our 'guests' was being visited by her deceased husband nightly. Her husband was telling her he preferred the shade of the large oak tree in the southeast corner of the cemetery to his current sunny location in the northeast corner. My first reaction was to snicker at the thought of his nightly visitation, imagining how the conversation may have gone:

> *Husband: "Hi, Hon, what are you doing?"*
> *Wife: "Trying to sleep!"*
> *Husband: "It's too hot here for me to sleep."*
> *Wife: "Oh my, you might not have been the perfect husband but I never thought you would be there!"*
> *Husband: "No, I meant it's hot because there is no shade on my side of the cemetery."*
> *Wife: "It serves you right – you should never have left me."*

But my mental wandering was interrupted and the smile rapidly faded from my face when the manager informed us he had agreed to have the gentleman moved to his new location the next day.

- Do we always strive to satisfy the customer despite the consequences it may mean for us?
- Do we act as if 'the customer is always right,' even if they aren't?

The cemetery opened at 8:00 am and since it was frowned upon to transport bodies while visitors were there - *I wasn't keen on moving him even if there was no one present* - we dug the new grave that afternoon to save time the next morning.

We then departed, agreeing to meet at 6:00 am to disinter our guest and help him change location. I went home to what turned out to be a sleepless night filled with visions from an overactive imagination, but my nightmares did not come close to what I actually experienced that day.

- Do we worry needlessly about what might happen, things out of our control, or do we enter our tasks with the confidence we can handle whatever comes our way?

Thankfully, the cemetery recently purchased a very small backhoe with an 18" shovel. Greg was the only one who knew how to operate it and when I arrived that morning he had it positioned at the foot of the grave. As he began digging, I prepared the new grave and then set out the items we would need to complete the transfer – shovels, straps, and a small tractor with a tiny trailer to move the body across the cemetery - next to where Greg was digging.

When Greg's backhoe shovel hit something hard, we knew we had reached the coffin; it was then Tom's and my turn. We jumped into the grave, one a little more enthusiastically than the other, and finished digging around the casket so we could slide the straps underneath it. The plan was to use the backhoe to lift the coffin out of the grave and on to the trailer.

- Do we understand the importance of contingency planning?

All was going well; the coffin, braced by the two straps on either side, was almost out of the grave when my heart stopped and my knees went to jelly! As the box was being raised, it split right in the middle, between the two straps, forming a perfect 'V.' The body slid out into the grave with the coffin following! It was just like the lullaby lyrics 'down will come baby, cradle and all.' As Greg tried to move the backhoe to prevent the casket's fall, he over-reacted and the shovel hit the side of the grave causing it, and the pile of dirt we had previously removed from the grave, to fall in on top of the poor gentleman. I could not take my eyes off the horrible scene in front of me!

When I recovered enough to look up, the first thing I noticed was that Tom had grabbed his shovel and was heading toward the grave. It was then I heard the screech of tires; when I turned in that direction, all I saw were the taillights of Greg's car headed out of the cemetery. I prayed that he was going for help, but I was wrong, for we didn't see him again until the next day.

Wanting nothing more than to go home, I looked at Tom in the grave alone, shoveling out the dirt. I knew I could not leave him. So I, too, entered the grave slowly, watching carefully where I stepped. I began helping Tom clear out the dirt, but I must admit that while he was taking large shovels full and throwing them over his shoulder, I was shoveling very gingerly. My sole intent was not to remove the dirt, but rather to avoid striking anything; for all I was removing with each shovel full I might as well have been using a teaspoon!

- Do we appreciate the value of teamwork?

After what seemed like an eternity, Tom hit part of the box. At that point, as if it were even possible, I became even more cautious in my task. We uncovered parts of the casket and removed them as they were found until we finally reached the body, which was now, after over a year in the grave, nothing but clothes draping a skeleton. It was then, as we slowly revealed the outline of the body, much like an archeologist on a dig, that Tom realized I was nervous. *(Thank you Captain Obvious!)* To help allay some of my fears he tried to distract me.

"Did you know that sometimes people hide money in their sock when they die?" he asked as he removed a sock. I guess it might be like the pharaohs who would bring supplies for their journey beyond.

- Do we recognize the value of humor, if used correctly, in a work environment?

When the body was partially free, I got out of the grave and was handed the two feet and legs. *I will never complain about wearing gloves when I work again!* I had to hold them out of the way while Tom finished freeing the rest of the body. I knelt at the side of the grave and when he was done, I took the body from Tom, laying it on the grass next to me as I was told to do. I then helped Tom out of the grave.

By now we were both sweating profusely from the effort. As I sat there trying to catch my breath, I was thinking that things could not get any worse. But once again I was wrong, for it was then I saw out of the corner of my eye, a car pulling into the cemetery. The accident at the gravesite had caused us to fall behind schedule. It was now after 8 am, and the cemetery was open! As I was about to panic, Tom turned to me and in a very calm voice clearly said, "Don't worry, just put the body in the grave."

Now here is when I did what many would call stupid but I like to call virtuous. Knowing how much that gentleman wanted to be buried under the tree, and recognizing that the grave next to us was no longer his home since we just 'evicted' him *(twice as a matter of fact)*, I jumped up, threw the skeleton over my right shoulder and ran as fast as I could across the cemetery to the oak tree.

I ran track in high school, so I could move quickly. I'm not sure if it was an adrenalin rush or the 'clankity-clank' I heard the entire time I was running, but, I am convinced that if there had been a timekeeper present I would have set a world record! When I reached my destination, I threw the body into the grave. *(Sorry, there was no thought of placing it, just of ending this nightmare.)*

- Do we commit to and fulfill our responsibilities in all that we do?

As I stood doubled over, my heart feeling as if it was going to pound itself right out of my chest, I realized as I stared into the new grave, that my adventure was far from over. While the skeleton was precisely placed in the middle of the grave there was one small problem. *It was missing its head!*

As I was about to involuntarily cease some bodily functions that were essential (like breathing), and start some not considered socially acceptable nor sanitary, I heard Tom calling me. I looked up to see him hobbling across the cemetery, hand held high over his head shouting, "You forgot something, Sonny!" He was holding the gentleman's skull!

I realized from that first summer job that I was destined for management; this revelation was not from a fear of getting my hands dirty, but rather because I had thousands of people under me and not one ever complained.

Seriously, though, there are a number of lessons I found valuable:

- We are capable of doing a lot more than we may think

- There are many things we cannot, or do not want, to do alone

- Teamwork plays an important role in being able to accomplish more than you think possible

- Things may and probably will not go as planned, so have contingency plans

Epilogue

The conclusion of the story is the widow came to the cemetery the next day and while she was there the manager summoned the three of us to meet with them. I felt like a child called to the principal's office, and went with much trepidation. When the woman told us her husband had spoken with her last night my head snapped up from staring at the floor, and I looked at her with eyes as big as saucers! Worried about what he might have told her, it took every bit of self-restraint to stop from crying out, "Don't believe him!" I was obviously and unexpectedly no longer skeptical about whether these visits actually occurred. She told us that he was very pleased with his new home and they both wanted to thank us for making him so happy. *I still believe my 'Phew' was audible, but thankfully no one ever mentioned it.*

Do we recognize:

- Meeting customer expectations and doing what you say you will do are extremely important?

- If things do not go as planned, if you work hard and have the right intentions, people are appreciative?

- To meet customer expectations stay calm and focused, especially when things go wrong and those around you are 'losing their heads' – it will reassure others and help you reach your ultimate goal!?

- There is no such thing as the perfect job – it is how *you* approach it and what *you* make of it?

Customer Fanatic

Thoughts on customer service

- "The goal as a company is to have customer service that is not just the best but legendary." - *Sam Walton, Founder of Wal-Mart*
- "If you build a great experience, customers tell each other about that. Word of mouth is very powerful." - *Jeff Bezos, CEO Amazon.com*
- "Customer satisfaction is worthless. Customer loyalty is priceless." - *Jeffrey Gitomer*
- "If you work just for money, you will never make it; but it you...put the customer first, success will be yours." – *Ray Kroc*

Ways leaders are customer fanatics

- Spend a lot of time talking to customers, face to face
- Focus on and involve your employees in improving the customer experience, how you make the customer feel when things go well and when they don't go according to expectation
- Notify customers when something goes wrong and explain the solution you are taking; act don't fret
- Empower employees to reward, compensate, and thank customers immediately and directly
- Learn about your customer, provide them solutions to problems they will encounter or service they will provide before they even know it exists
- Design your processes based on customer needs
- Strive for continuous improvement in your own operations; be easy to work with; partner with customers, employees and vendors/suppliers
- Have contingency plans just in case

Diversity

[dih-**vur**-si-tee, dahy-]:

...the quality or condition of having or being composed of many different elements, forms, types, ideas, etc., especially the state of having people who are different races or who have different cultures in a group or organization

Synonyms: assortment, heterogeneity
Antonyms: sameness, similarity

Leadership Is...

Diversity

My wife is a great cook. That is not the reason I married her, but it didn't hurt. I must admit, it has been a very pleasant added benefit because as much as she loves to cook, I love to eat!

Having been raised on Ring Dings and Ho Hos, I am an admitted chocoholic, and just for the record, I do not consider fruit a dessert. I would rather risk a doctor visit than eat an apple a day.

It is surprising, then, that one of my favorite desserts is my wife's French Apple Pie. Besides the apples, there are far too many things that this picky eater will not normally allow past his lips, even if you paid me; cinnamon is a perfect example. And what about the other ingredients? Raw flour is tasteless, boring and would cause almost anyone to choke. Olive Oil? I associate that with his horrid brother, Castor; need I say more? A raw egg? It was part of my Fraternity initiation and I can assure you, when consumed can make many gag. And sugar? While this may be my favorite, if I get too much of it, it just makes me sick.

So why do I love Gayle's French Apple Pie so much? I think it is because she includes the ingredients in the proper quantities and at the proper times to make magic. She does not measure precisely; there are variables that she carefully considers and adjusts as she goes. She has taken the skill of cooking and turned it into an art!

But I think the ultimate success is affected by the environment and process as well as the ingredients. She painstakingly stirs, sifts, blends and heats with precision, bringing out the best in all the flavors combined. If you don't belive me, then the next time you make a pie, leave out one of the ingredients, or don't blend or whisk when required and see how it tastes. When Gayle is done with her pie, the result is a product 'to die for.'

Do you produce a product 'to die for' at work? If not, it may be good to ask yourself, do I;

- Recognize the enormous 'ingredients' available, the talents of every employee on the team?
- Involve them all, no matter how I feel about them personally, to produce the best solution or product?
- Monitor and adjust as we proceed, rather than predeterme the mix of 'ingredients'?
- Nurture and prepare them to create an environment that will allow all their 'flavors' (talents) to blend perfectly to ensure success?

Oh, there is one other reason my wife's French Apple Pie is better than any dessert I have ever eaten. It is because she takes pride in her work and wants to do her best, but more importantly, it is because she loves me!

- Do you take pride in your work?
- Do your employees and peers know you care about them?

If you do and they do, it will make a world of difference – in the result and in the way their taste buds are prepared for what is to come.

Diversity

Thoughts on diversity

- "We need diversity of thought … to face new challenges." – *Tim Berners-Lee, Physicist*
- "…diversity makes for a rich tapestry, and … all the threads of the tapestry are equal in value …" – *Maya Angelou, American Poet*

Ways leaders practice diversity

- Provide diversity training and awareness for everyone
- Practice fair hiring practices; do not let biases get involved
- Provide 'affinity' groups to promote and increase awareness
- Establish diverse project teams to address issues and problems
- Recognize and reward diversity behaviors
- Be consistent in performance review and career development opportunities
- Ensure leadership roles are made available to all qualified
- Hold events that promote and educate on diversity
- Establish policies that allow for diverse cultural needs
- Enforce policies as guidelines to accommodate specific circumstance
- Participate in local events supporting diversity
- Join a community outreach organization
- Measure and report on diversity actions and compliance regularly

Preparation

[prep-*uh*-rey-sh*uh n*]:

...the action or process of getting ready for some use, service, occasion, test or duty

Synonym: groundwork, homework
Antonym: unaware, napping

Leadership Is...

Preparation

Acting can be a glamorous profession. The satisfaction of making people believe your character is real and feel the character's emotions is most gratifying. The adoring fans and the fame one garners enhances your ego and self-worth. Oh, and the money isn't half bad either. Unfortunately, though, for every successful actor, there are thousands who never fulfill their dreams. An actor friend shared with me this story of how hard it is to make it into 'Show Biz.'

One struggling actor, try as he might, could not break into the movies in California so he moved to New York City to see if he would have better luck getting on Broadway. He was very young, just out of college, with a drama degree and very few connections. He knew he would have to make it on his own, so he took a job waiting tables at the Stardust Diner on the corner of Broadway and 51st Street. If you have never been there, it is worth a stop when you are in the City, not for the food, which is good, but for the entertainment. The entire staff is comprised of aspiring actors who sing and dance continuously throughout the meal. It was there this young man got his first break!

- Do we seek options when we are faced with obstacles?

A new play was opening in three months and there was a small part which had not yet been filled. The Director saw him at the diner, thought he had the right 'look,' and offered him the role. It was only one line at the beginning of the show, but it was critical in that it served as a prelude to the entire play. The play was already being touted as a smash hit, a potential Tony Award winner, so while it was a small part, he knew it would give him great exposure and could launch his career. He jumped at the opportunity!

- Are we afraid to take on 'menial' roles for future growth and opportunity?

The line was relatively simple: "Hark, I hear the sound of a gunshot disturbing the still of the night!" It was the first line of the show, occurring even before the curtain went up, and because it did not involve interaction with any other character, the Director told him he did not need to come to the rehearsals, just show up on opening night.

The young man knew this was a chance of a lifetime, so for the next 3 months he did nothing but practice his line, "Hark, I hear the sound of a gunshot disturbing the still of the night!" He practiced every conceivable way to say those 14 words, emphasizing different words, emphasizing multiple words, using different cadences, using varied tones and loudness. He practiced his posture, his hand motions, his facial expressions; he even practiced different strides to walk on to the stage. About 2 weeks before the premiere, sounding like Professor Henry Higgins talking to Eliza Doolittle in My Fair Lady, he exclaimed, "By Jove, I think I've got it!" Those last two weeks were spent perfecting his delivery – "Hark, I hear the sound of a gunshot disturbing the still of the night!" The tone, inflection and elocution were perfect; he had done it so many times that it now became second nature to him. He was ready!

- Do we put in the time and personal commitment to ensure we will get the desired results?

Opening night finally arrived. His parents were there, seated in the 4th row. They were waiting to see their son's debut; they would not have missed it for the world. The actor was pacing backstage, arms flailing, his lips moving silently as he practiced his line, "Hark, I hear the sound of a gunshot disturbing the still of the night!"

Then it was time; the music stopped, the lights faded. The actor began slowly walking across the stage in front of the dark curtains. Every movement was exactly as he had practiced, and the audience was mesmerized by his presence. Yes, he had nailed his entrance! The practice was worth it.

With the dim spotlight on him, the actor stepped up to his mark to deliver his line when -- BANG! -- a loud noise rang out from behind the curtain.

The actor jumped at the noise, his eyes growing wide and his head turning in all directions as he screamed out, "What the heck was that?"

- Do we recognize the importance of the context in which we lead and act?

- Do we only consider our own roles and agendas, or do we take into consideration those of others in preparing for meetings and discussions?

- Are we prepared for the unexpected? Failure to do so may be a career limiting move, no matter what your profession.

Preparation

Thoughts on preparation

- "By failing to prepare, you are preparing to fail." – *Benjamin Franklin*
- "Today's preparation determines tomorrow's achievement." – *Anonymous*
- "Hope for the best, prepare for the worst." – *Chris Bradford, The Ring of Earth*

Ways leaders prepare

- Be a voracious reader; learn as much as possible
- Consider the consequences on areas other than the one being worked on
- Always ask 'what if' to explore all possibilities
- It is okay to be negative; look for those things that can go wrong; poke holes in plans until improved
- Prepare contingency plans
- Consider resources and abilities, not just cost
- Define steps and milestones
- Assign people to activities (based on skill, passion, growth opportunity)
- Report on progress (to team and management) regularly
- Hold people accountable for their areas of responsibility

Appreciation

[*uh*-pree-shee-**ey**-sh*uh*]:

...an expression of admiration, approval, or gratitude in recognition of the demonstration of a desired behavior or a significant result

Synonyms: gratitude, thanks
Antonyms: rudeness, ingratitude

Leadership Is...

Appreciation

I did not personally know either of the gentlemen in this story, but I did have the honor and privilege to work with the daughter of one of the men during my time in the Latin America and Caribbean Region at FedEx Express. Knowing Vera, I am not the least bit surprised by the caring, generosity and kindness that her father, Fred, displayed. Here is his story:

Fred had a small teak farm in Costa Rica many years ago; he had a caretaker who lived on the property in a small rickety wooden house without electricity and with no running water. He was about 70 years old and very wiry, a hard working 'campesino' (farmer.)

It was because of this man that Fred was able to move to the United States after establishing his business. The caretaker was completely trustworthy, extremely loyal and, as mentioned above, had an impeccable work ethic. Fred had no second thoughts about leaving this man in charge of his farm.

After a few years in the States, Fred decided to show his appreciation for this man's dedication to him and his family, so, on one of his visits, he equipped the man's shack with electricity. That evening, at dusk, when the worker came home, Fred was at the cabin with the lights on, beaming about how his dedicated worker and his family could now see as clear as day regardless of the time. He thought of how much this would mean to his trusted friend and was so proud to have improved this old man's life!

- Do we remember to thank people for what they mean to and do for us and others?

Three months later, on his next quarterly visit, Fred went down to the house one evening to see his caretaker and, much to his surprise, he found his home in total darkness! Wondering if something had gone wrong with the electrical connection, he asked, "What happened to the lights." The caretaker unabashedly said, "I couldn't sleep so I had to take the damn light bulbs out!"

- Do we satisfactorily explain and educate others as to the purpose of change?

- During change, do we satisfactorily prepare others so they can embrace it and the change can achieve its desired effect?

For an old man who was used to rising with the rooster's crow and going to bed when the sun goes down, electricity was wasteful and an inconvenience, but Fred, now fully Americanized, never thought twice about whether or not what he was doing was good; he was sure it was!

- Do we take into account what others want to be sure the 'thank you,' or any of our actions, is meaningful?

What was intended as a positive turned out to be an action by 'management' that could have destroyed the relationship.

Appreciation

Thoughts on appreciation

- "... a person's greatest emotional need is to feel appreciated." – *H. Jackson Brown*
- "When I was a kid, there was no collaboration; it's you ... bossing your friends around. But as an adult, (it) is all about appreciating the talents of the people you surround yourself with and knowing you could never have made (it) by yourself." – *Steven Spielberg*

Ways leaders appreciate

- Remember employees names and those of their family members
- Visit people on their 'own turf'; manage by walking around
- Look for the good things people do and praise them immediately
- Remember birthdays and anniversaries; send cards; make calls
- Hold special events in the department for celebrating success
- Sponsor/support employee special interests
- Highlight employees in a regularly published newsletter
- Ask employees to train or teach others
- Give employees leadership on major projects
- Provide them visibility at senior levels
- Say thank you
- Have an 'open door' policy and listen to understand
- Send notes of appreciation to employee's family members

Focus

[**foh**-k*uh* s]:

...a main purpose or interest; a central point, as of attraction, attention, or activity

Synonyms: emphasis, concentration, aim
Antonyms: blur, make unclear

Leadership Is...

Focus

When I first started at the company, I was much younger and had far less responsibilities than I do now, so when I got an opportunity to travel, I loved it! It not only made me feel important but it also gave me the chance to see places I could not, and as experience later taught me, I would not necessarily want to see on my own.

Like most newcomers to the workforce, I did not own a sufficient business wardrobe to make it a week on the road. So, like others, I learned how to pack two neutral color dress shirts to alternate with two pairs of dress pants. One pair of slacks belonged to my only suit. The suit jacket doubled as a sports coat. Two ties were more than satisfactory.

- Do we plan and organize to maximize efficiency and provide the greatest flexibility?

I also learned the secret of keeping things looking pressed while on the road, despite having been crammed in a suitcase or previously worn on the trip. One thing this did not involve, however, was an iron. I don't recall many ironing boards or irons when I traveled in my early years. Maybe this was because I never wanted to find one because I had no idea how to use an iron anyway. The trick was simple - merely hang your clothes in the bathroom and turn the shower on hot. As you probably know, the result is a 'steam pressed' garment.

On one out of town venture, a less experienced traveling companion had a suit that needed pressing for the last day of our trip, so I shared with him the road-warrior secret. He was most appreciative and after a late dinner, he proceeded to his room to de-wrinkle his suit before going to bed.

My wake-up call was set for 6:30 so when my phone rang at 5:00 a.m., I was confused. After answering it, my confusion turned to fear. My coworker was on the line screaming for me to come to his room immediately. Acting on adrenalin, I threw on pants and made my way down the hall in a matter of seconds.

When I got there he informed me he could not get into the bathroom. As I reached for the handle, he shouted a warning - slightly too late. The handle was burning hot! As it turned out, he had hung up his suit and turned the hot water on after dinner, just as I had suggested. He did admit getting distracted, first doing a little work, then watching an interesting TV show and finally nodding off during the news. He fell asleep and just now awoke to this disaster!

We finally got the door open with the help of a towel he had in his room. The hot steam was oppressive. We could not see anything. We finally worked our way to the shower and turned off the water. When the fog cleared, we saw his suit, still hanging where he had left it. It was absolutely soaked and, most definitely, not wearable - as if that needed to have been said.

But that was not the worst of it, for what we saw next left us gaping in horror! As we stood in the middle of the bathroom and looked around, no matter what wall we looked at, all we saw was the wallpaper peeled and drooping halfway down!

- Do we have a plan and just assume that because we have one, it will be implemented correctly?
- Do we let things distract us from our purpose and our people, no matter how well intentioned we are?
- Are we are so concerned about our immediate objective that we lose site of the bigger picture and what the impact of our actions might be?

As far as the ending of the story goes, suffice it to say that when I met my coworker at the station, he wasn't wearing a jacket and had on the same pants as the day before. I never asked what he did about the situation and he never volunteered. All I can say, though, is I'm pretty sure there was a puddle of water under his dripping suitcase when I stored my suitcase next to his at the station.

Focus

Thoughts on staying focused

- "My success, part of it certainly, is that I have focused in on a few things." — *Bill Gates*
- "A person who aims at nothing is sure to hit it." – *Anonymous*
- "If you see a bandwagon, it's too late." – *James Goldsmith*

Ways leaders keep focus

- Establish and publicize goals; the more people know about them the greater commitment you will have to completion of them
- Concentrate on the positives, not the negatives
- Keep the end in sight; avoid distractions
- Document specific steps that will be followed to reach a goal and refer to it often; eat the elephant a bite at a time
- Reward (yourself and others) when milestones are met
- If projected results will not lead to the desired or a positive result, 'abort' the effort quickly regardless of the expenditures to date
- Involve others (including the customer) on the team to monitor progress
- Remain flexible; work and adjust the plan as necessary

Courage

[**kur**-ij, **kuhr**]:

...the ability to do something that you know is difficult or dangerous

Synonyms: bravery, valor, guts
Antonyms: cowardice, fear, timidity

Leadership Is...

Courage

What is leadership? When this question, was first posed to me, I immediately thought of Emma, my special needs granddaughter, and how my responsibilities for her are fraught with the same fears a leader in any organization may face. Both roles come with tremendous responsibilities and one can't help wondering if we have the capabilities, if we are doing enough or if we are making a difference.

Rather than being consumed by the negatives we encounter - or the 'what-ifs' we imagine - we must remain focused on what _we_ can do - and act accordingly. We must 'keep the main thing the main thing' and do our best at all times, especially those that are the most difficult. Success is only achieved when we give the very best of what we have and who we are.

The greatest role any of us can play is one that makes a positive difference in someone else's life. As a manager and leader, we have the opportunity to do that daily. I wrote this short poem a few years ago as a reminder to me and the family to help us through our struggles, and although it is about my relationship with Emma and is deeply personal, I felt it important to share. For it not only illustrates how we all can make a difference, it teaches us a lesson in courage as well. Lessons that apply to our personal and business lives equally.

A Difference

Uncomfortable in every way, I'm scared to death of the awesome responsibility that rests upon my shoulders.

The responsibility for someone locked in a shell with no way out.

With no way for me or anyone else to understand her needs, her wishes, her desires, her dreams.

Never thinking I am doing enough, never thinking I am making a difference.

But then, a squeal of joy when I enter the room as she hears my voice.

The happiness expressed by the sparkle in her eyes when I talk with her.

The calm she feels, even in her discomfort, when she is in my care.

The gifts she gives - the smile, the laughter, yes, even the tears are expressions of love she feels for me.

A love that goes beyond all expectations and beyond all reason.

It is a love that fills my heart with joy! It is then my discomfort pales in comparison with hers.

And I understand, *she* is the one leading by example, not me. It is her need, appreciation and love that inspire me

And compel me to never forget that we all make a difference -

Just by being who we are.

For those of you who do not know her, Emma was born with special needs due to a severe mitochondrial disease. Her life expectancy was two years. Emma was nine when this poem was written. She reached that age in part because of the love, care and courage of my son and daughter-in-law, but mostly because of Emma herself. She refused to give up. When written, it was a struggle for Emma to breathe almost every minute of every day.

Like Emma, we face many obstacles and challenges as we go through life; we learn from each. Sometimes we learn our greatest lessons from the most unexpected sources; in my case, I have learned more about courage from Emma in her short 9 years than I have from anyone else.

Looking at her, I know there is no challenge too big for me to take on, no challenge we cannot overcome if we have the strength to do so. We have to have the courage to know ourselves, our desires and our dreams and not be afraid of pursuing them. And because Emma and I love each other as we do, we give each other the strength to go on.

Epilogue

A few weeks after this was written, Emma passed away. Although she is not with us physically, she is still and will always remain with us. We will always remember the lessons in love, courage and leadership she taught us. We are blessed to have had her in our lives.

Courage

Thoughts on courage

- "...courage (is) not the absence of fear, but the triumph over it. The brave man is not he who does not feel afraid, but he who conquers that fear." – *Nelson Mandela*
- "Without courage, wisdom bears no fruit." – *Baltasar Gracian*
- "I am not funny. What I am is brave." – *Lucille Ball*

Ways leaders display courage

- Provide meaningful employee feedback – good and bad in a timely manner
- Allow employees to make mistakes but take responsibility for any that occur
- Speak up at meetings
- Tell management if they may not be headed in the right direction or may be able to do something better
- Encourage and allow employees to provide feedback freely
- Conduct 360 degree performance reviews on themselves, including reviews from employees all the way 'down' the organization chart and from customers
- Say "I am sorry" or "I made a mistake" when they were wrong
- Take on difficult projects; assume greater responsibilities
- Delegate to others

Communication

[k*uh*-myoo-ni-**key**-sh*uh* n]:

...the imparting or exchanging of thoughts, opinions, ideas or information by orally, visually, or in writing through a common system of symbols, signs, or behaviors

Synonyms: message, exchange
Antonyms: silence, secrecy

Leadership Is...

Communication

New York City is unique, offering something for everyone – sports, shopping, entertainment, history, food – making it a Mecca for tourists.

One evening, a man was walking back to his hotel after seeing the 'hottest' show on Broadway; he was singing one of its songs in his head and thinking how lucky he was to get a ticket on such short notice! Maybe because he was distracted, maybe because it was late, maybe because the traffic was heavy with cars jockeying for position – whatever the reason, as the man crossed one of the larger streets in the City, he was struck by a taxi.

He was seriously hurt; he was lying motionless in the street, bleeding heavily. Traffic was stopped and a large crowd gathered around him, most too scared or unequipped to help. Within minutes, however, a young policeman broke through the crowd to establish control and determine what needed to be done. He realized quickly that even though the man was conscious, his injuries were life threatening and there was a very good chance the man would not survive.

The Officer called 911 and bent down to comfort the man until the ambulance arrived. Noticing the cross hanging around the man's neck, he stood up and shouted to the crowd, "We need a Priest. Is anyone a Priest?" No one answered, so he shouted more loudly, "I need a Priest!"

The crowd grew still, but finally an older gentleman timidly pushed his way through the crowd to the Officer. He was dressed shabbily; he was unkempt. The Policeman looked him up and down and asked him quizzically, with disbelief, "Are you a Priest?" The older man answered apologetically, not taking his eyes off the pavement, "No I am not. But since no one else came forward, I thought maybe I could help." Pointing to a large cathedral near-by he continued, "I may not be a Priest, but I have lived outside that Catholic Church on the corner for over 32 years. I have heard every word they said in the Church during that time so I thought maybe I could use what I have heard to help comfort the man."

The Officer looked around the crowd and realizing there was no one else stepping forward, thanked the elderly gentleman and asked him to go ahead. With difficulty, the gentleman knelt down next to the injured tourist. He took the man's hand gently in his. He looked around, composing his thoughts and tried to recall just the right words, those words that seemed to make the congregation most appreciative.

After a few moments, he leaned over the man, and with the utmost respect and compassion he could muster, he began, "B-7, I-18, N-32, G-56, O-64."

- Are we effectively communicating with our peers, customers and employees?

- Do we make our messages clear?

- Do we communicate with just words but no meaning?

Learning manifests itself in actions and results; nothing is learned until it is applied properly. And true learning cannot be accomplished through communication alone; it must also include an understanding of the context in which it applies.

Communication

Thoughts on communication

- "The single biggest problem in communication is the illusion that it has taken place." – *George Bernard Shaw*
- "The most important thing in communication is to hear what isn't being said." – *Peter Drucker*
- "The basic building block of communication is the feeling every human being is unique and of value." – *Anonymous*

Ways leaders communicate effectively

- Listen actively, asking questions to understand, not just to hear
- Use 'simple' words to facilitate understanding
- Communicate frequently, telling people what will be said, telling them, and then telling them what was told
- Reinforce messages through actions
- Treat everyone with respect and dignity
- Inject humor when and as appropriate
- Constantly seek input; ask for everyone to share their views
- Seek informal leaders to carry the message 'up and down'
- Be brief
- Share good news and bad

Facilitation

[f*uh*-sil-i-**tey**-sh*uh* n]:

...the increasing of the ease or intensity of a response by repeated stimulation

Synonyms: enablement, acceleration
Antonym: preventing

Leadership Is…

Facilitation

If I asked you to name the best basketball player in the NBA over the last 10 years I'm sure your response would include names like Kobe Bryant, LeBron James, and maybe a few others, but the list would probably be relatively short.

While I am not an avid basketball fan, as a Memphian I would be lying if I didn't admit to being excited about the Grizzlies at the start of the 2010-2011 season. And I am not alone for the entire city went bonkers. The Grizz have long been the doormat of the NBA playoffs, when, at one point, they held a perfect record — 0 wins in 12 games. But something magical happened to them the next year, even without a big name star.

What they had obtained, however, was a player who started playing basketball at age 13 and graduated High School with a 3.96 GPA. He was a Duke graduate and named the National Collegiate Player of the Year in 2001. That same year he was a 1st round draft pick. This individual definitely had the background to be an NBA star, but I would bet dollars to donuts that none of you had him on your list of the top basketball players.

The question is: why wouldn't anyone have mentioned Shane Battier as the best basketball player during that time span? It's probably because his point totals were not that impressive. Some may say that makes him a failure or a disappointment, but that couldn't be further from the truth. Just ask any NBA player or coach during the early part of the century who they would want on their team, and Shane's name would have been at the top of their list.

That's because every team Shane has ever played on found a way to win. They did so because he was a true leader. He made everyone on his team better. He was unselfish and did what was best for the team, not himself. He not only knew his teammates' strengths and weaknesses but adapted *his game* to enhance their strengths and to protect their weaknesses. Shane did everything to make his teammates shine. He walked the talk and was not satisfied with the status quo. His positive attitude was contagious. Just one look at the FedEx Forum that year, an 'echo chamber' for most of the previous seasons suddenly filled beyond capacity with towel waving, screaming fans!

Shane's return to the Grizzlies was miraculous. The Grizzlies made the playoffs; they not only won their first playoff game that year with Shane, but as the eighth-seed team they went on to defeat the number one seed, the San Antonio Spurs, in 6 games. Thirty six hours later, in Oklahoma City, the score of the first game in the second round was Grizzlies 114 - Thunder 101. Shane's presence made a positive difference to the team and to the city that no one can deny. Shane retired in 2014 from the Miami Heat, a key part of a back-to-back championship team; he will be missed, for he continued to make a difference in every game in which he played.

The Grizzlies' confidence and culture have been changed for the good, in a large part due to the leadership of Shane Battier; this culture of teamwork has carried them forward for years to come. Zach Randolph is being called unstoppable. Tony Allen is truly the 'Grindfather.' The other Gasol brother, Marc, says, "It's winning time. This is who we are. We're going to win or lose being who we are." And who they are can be defined by their complete and unwavering commitment to teamwork.

Shane Battier is a role model for us all; he shows us that leadership does not always come from the star, that leadership appears in many different forms and almost always makes the whole greater than the sum of its parts. He is living proof that leadership starts with one's own values - that *leadership comes from within*. It is an outward and visible sign of an inward and spiritual grace.

Facilitation

Thoughts on facilitation

- "Be the change you wish to see..." – *Mahatma Gandhi*
- "We miss more by not seeing than by not knowing." – *Sir William Osler*
- "...the best facilitators allow the solution to be defined and owned by the individuals they are facilitating..." – *Bob Zimmerman*

Ways leaders facilitate

- Defines the objective clearly, keeps it 'top of mind' but allows some straying to generate new ideas
- Allows and encourages (requires) input from everyone
- Keeps the interest and energy high
- Removes obstacles to career progression or project completion through networking, knowledge, funding,...
- Asks 'what if' questions
- Keeps meetings and direction positive
- Allows individuals to choose and work on their particular passion
- Documents to ensure accountability
- Follows up and acts

Networking

[**net**-wur-king]:

...the exchange of information or services among individuals, groups, or institutions; *specifically*: the cultivation of productive relationships for employment or business

Synonyms: interacting, exchanging
Antonyms: soloing, acting alone

Leadership Is…

Networking

This weekend, my wife Gayle and I visited a small rural town in Mississippi known as Water Valley. It's the proud home of the Watermelon Festival! We met some very interesting people there. Among them were two independent filmmakers who met in Africa and were filming in the area, and a woman born in South Germany who admired Faulkner so much she moved to Water Valley and took a job at Ole Miss in Oxford, MS, Faulkner's home. Perhaps the most interesting person we met, however, was 'Mr. Bob,' whom we first saw waving frantically at us to come in as we peeked through the window of the local pharmacy and soda fountain. He was seated at a table enjoying a 35 cent cup of coffee and a conversation with an old friend.

We later learned that Mr. Bob, as he was affectionately called, was known by everyone in town, and it was not surprising that we met him at the soda fountain. Mr. Bob was about 80 years old, and was married for over 50 years to his wife who he described proudly as the most wonderful woman in the world. He told us he ruled the roost at his house now, but then added it was only because his wife had recently been moved to a nursing home nearby. He assured us that when he went to visit her there, however, she most definitely was in charge. You could tell by the way he told us this, he loved every minute of his time with her!

But this isn't a story about Mr. Bob, but rather it is about a story he told us, and probably every other friend and acquaintance he has ever had. He told this story as if it were Water Valley folk-lore.

He started out by telling us that Water Valley is a very small town, where everyone knows everyone else, where friends help out friends, and strangers, too.

- Do we recognize and appreciate a strong network and the value it can provide?

He then told us of a middle-aged couple, high school sweethearts, who were married for about 15 years, he thought. The woman walked into the pharmacy and Mr. Bob related the conversation between the pharmacist and the women, which went something like this:

The woman: "I want to buy some arsenic."

The pharmacist, thinking that the woman perhaps did not know what she was requesting and was asking for the wrong thing: "Do you know that arsenic is a poison?"

The woman: "Yes, I do. I need some poison."

The pharmacist, trying to determine if there was something else he could provide that would help her: "I am not allowed to sell you a poison. Why do you want it?"

The woman: "I want to kill my husband."

The pharmacist, taken aback because he has known this kind-hearted woman and her husband both, having gone to school with them: "What?! Why would you want to kill your husband?"

The woman, calmly: "Because I caught him cheating on me with another woman."

The pharmacist, trying to make sure she did not do anything rash: "Are you sure?"

The woman: "Oh, I am sure. I saw them together."

The pharmacist, incredulous that this occurred: "Maybe you are mistaken?"

The woman: "No mistake. I am certain. I have a picture of them to prove it."

With that, she took a picture out of her purse and handed it to the pharmacist, who immediately recognized the woman's husband in a very compromising position. A moment later, the pharmacist, suppressing a gasp, recognized the woman in the picture - his wife!

As he turned back to the woman, handing her the picture, the pharmacist calmly said: "Oh, I didn't know you had a prescription for that."

- Do we identify and build allies before 'selling' an idea or action?

- Do we recognize that the best results are achieved through commitment, not compliance, through personalization rather than generalization?

- Do we act with conviction when we are confronted with facts?

Leaders have confidence in themselves to make difficult decisions, which in turn, inspires others to act and achieve their goals as well. This confidence, in self and others, is trust; trust is earned, essential and oh, so perishable. Don't risk losing it.

Disclaimer: The author, in no way, supports or condones the actions of the fictionalized characters portrayed in this story. But I do appreciate the lessons that can be learned from retelling it as it was passed on to me. It also reminds us of another important moral dilemma we all have faced:

Do/should we allow the end to justify the means?

Networking

Thoughts on networking

- "I like to define networking as cultivating mutually beneficial, give-and-take, win-win relationships..." – *Bob Burg*
- "The richest people in the world look for and build networks, everyone else looks for work." – *Robert Kiyosaki*

Ways leaders network

- Build relationships/partnerships both up and down the organization
- Provide benefit to others; 'give before you get'
- Join and/or lead relevant outside organizations at work, in the industry and throughout the community
- Stay in touch with others regularly
- Jot down notes about networking partners to remember significant facts
- Respect the time of others, be brief
- Be nice
- Differentiate yourself in some way (knowledge, network, responsiveness...)
- Follow up on your commitments and promises
- Always speak in a positive manner; be optimistic and energetic
- Carry and distribute business cards; collect them and sort then appropriately
- Be precise and specific

Feedback

[**feed**-bak]:

...helpful information or criticism that is given to someone to say what can be done to improve a performance, product, etc.

Synonyms: advice, response
Antonyms: indifference, uncaring

Leadership Is...

Feedback

I love FedEx! Now don't get me wrong; I didn't go there thinking it would be an ideal job. As a matter of fact, I actually was running away from a job rather than running to one, something I strongly discourage people from doing. But I was fortunate to find out early that this was the place for me; I remember it well.

It came as a result of my first high leverage project - to determine the new delivery commitment time for FedEx. The delivery commitment at the time was next day close of business. Having graduated and worked as an Industrial Engineer, this was something I thought I could do but it was most definitely not something I was comfortable with because I had never experienced anything like it in terms of size, scope and importance. If that wasn't bad enough, I was on my own, knowing that in two months I had to report my findings to Mr. Smith, our founder and CEO.

- Do we trust our team members enough to give them not just important projects, but projects critical to our success, projects that stretch their abilities, without standing over them every minute?

When I was through, Mr. Smith had a 200+ page report (most was the appendix) that covered every conceivable delivery commitment time between 8am and 5pm. It included analyses of the people needed, the vehicles, the potential impact on volume, the facility changes required, and much more. When I presented it, I was proud of the detail and documentation I was able to gather, analyze, assimilate and present. I was confident that my recommendation of a noon delivery commitment was the right one. This was further strengthened when, after presenting the findings and recommendation, Mr. Smith himself thanked me and commended me on the level of detail.

A few weeks later, I was fortunate to be invited to the meeting at which Mr. Smith was to announce our new delivery commitment. Given this honor, my confidence grew; I was sure that I had done a stellar job and that within the hour Mr. Smith would be announcing that Federal Express was again raising the bar with a new 12:00pm delivery commitment! Why else would I be invited?

- Do we recognize the value of our employees/team by sharing the accolades with them?

Not minding sitting along the back wall, as was the custom for staff at our senior officers' meetings, I was on pins and needles! My first major project at a new company, with CEO/Founder visibility; what could be better! As I was debating how to react to them announcing my recommended delivery commitment, Mr. Smith stood, addressed the senior management team, and announced our new commitment - 10:30 am!

I was incredulous, beginning to feel discouraged and under-appreciated. My thoughts then went to those of inadequacy, and then quickly to thoughts on whether I needed to look for a job in another company. But what happened next was totally unexpected, and may be considered the turning point in my career.

Mr. Smith, a busy man as you can imagine, came over to speak with me after the meeting. He smiled at me, shook my hand, and thanked me personally for a job well done. And then he provided me with some valuable feedback which I have never forgotten. He reiterated the high quality of work I provided and the value it gave him in making his decision, but he also told me that there was one piece of the analysis I was not able to evaluate - the ability of our competitor, UPS, to match the delivery time we adopted. He felt UPS could match a noon commitment within 18 months but it would take up to 3 years to match the 10:30 time and, by then, we would have firmly established our niche/position in the market.

- Are we courageous enough to make difficult decisions with the facts available to us?
- Do we accept what is given to us as 'gospel,' or do we ask further questions, delve deeper to gather additional relevant information before making a decision?

This whole process took no more than 30 seconds but its impact lasted a lifetime. It created what I hope FedEx considers a valuable 35 year employee; it helped me to consistently look for and see the big picture, not just my area of expertise. What could have been a crushing blow to the ego turned into an immeasurable positive! It was the beginning of my understanding of what a great leader does at all levels of the business. It helped shape my career.

- Do we provide people with positive feedback as well as constructive advice that allows them to feel good about themselves and to want to continue to grow?

- Do we recognize their need to feel valued?

In my case the experience, especially the 30 second 'After Action Review,' made me know I was valued and appreciated. It made me a loyal 'FedEx-er'!

Feedback

Thoughts on feedback

- "We all need people who will give us feedback. That's how we improve." - *Bill Gates*
- "Feedback is the breakfast of champions." – *Ken Blanchard*
- "Regular feedback is one of the hardest things to drive through an organization." - *Kenneth Chenault*

Ways leaders provide positive feedback

- Give immediate praise for positive behaviors and guidance for negative behaviors
- Focus on behavior not results
- Provide feedback that is very specific
- Provide feedback often
- "Spread it around' to all
- Separate emotion from techniques; avoid judgmental comments
- Take a more positive approach to giving beginners (new hires) negative feedback; they need encouragement so as not to be disheartened
- Be more direct with confident, experienced employees when giving negative feedback
- Build off a positive and work from there
- Create a 'buddy system' to provide coaching rather than feedback
- Establish and clearly define goals and follow up often

Adaptability

[*uh*-**dap**-t*uh*-bi*h*l i-tee]:

...being able to change or be changed in order to fit or work better in some situation or for some purpose

Synonym: flexibility
Antonyms: rigidity, unchangeable

Leadership Is...

Adaptability

I don't like to swim. Well, that's not exactly true. The fact is, I can't swim, which takes all the fun out of it and perhaps is the reason I don't like it! When I get in the water every muscle in my body tenses to the point that I have been told I resemble Dr. Frankenstein's creation trying to move. Others have said I look like a cat right before it hits a bathtub, arms and legs spread out in every direction, eyes wide, hair standing straight up in the air, and emitting an eerie scream!

I am not proud of this but I want you to know my failure to swim is not due to a lack of trying. I took two full semesters of swimming at college to no avail.

One thing I am proud of, though, is that my children never knew this until they were much older and were swimming themselves. I even helped teach them to swim; there was no reason not to, I had enough lessons to know what was supposed to be done even if I could not do it myself. The most ironic part is me sitting on the edge of the pool while they dove off the high dive, saying "you'll come get me daddy, if I need you" and me assuring them I would. I know I would have found a way if I had to, but thank goodness it was never necessary. I did have a backup plan; the lifeguard was on full alert!

- Do we allow every individual to see their potential, encouraging them to achieve it without 'weighing them down' with our own limitations?

But this story is about a family spring vacation in Breckenridge, Colorado. The family decided to go on a level 3 white river rafting trip. It obviously was not my idea but I agreed to go after being assured by the guide that level 3 was not dangerous. Everyone was excited, well almost everyone, as we got our pre-trip instructions. There were six people per raft, 3 on a side; it was our job to provide the muscle power to paddle our way down the river. There was also an experienced guide in the rear to steer. Our experienced guide was a recent Harvard graduate who told us this was his full time job.

At one point during the pre-trip instructions, I began to have serious second thoughts. Our guide was explaining what we were to do in the event someone fell out of the raft! He emphasized how cold the water was and that someone falling in would only have about one minute before they would lose consciousness from the cold. I looked around hoping someone else would want to change their mind, but they were eating this up. He went on to say if it should occur, our job was to paddle as hard as we could until we were slightly ahead of the person, at which time he would holler at the person closest to the recalcitrant traveler to drop the paddle, lean over, grab the person by the top of the life vest and pull him/her on top of you as you fell backwards into the middle of the raft. As we started on our journey, my parting words to the family were to hold on, as I checked and rechecked my life vest and slid my feet into the floor straps, tightening them until all circulation was cut off to my toes.

- Do we recognize the importance of contingency plans and the clear communication and implementation of these to our team?

The first fifteen minutes of the trip went so well I actually began breathing again. It was then, however, that we went through a bend and our river merged with another. I think I heard it before I saw it. The water was rushing so fast from the melting snow on the mountains that it was traveling faster than I drive my car, hitting rocks and spraying water everywhere. My sphincter muscle began to tighten even more when I heard the guide mutter a four letter word softly, almost inaudibly. I knew this could not be good.

The next 10 minutes were hell for me. We were hit by one large wave after another; I knew better, but I swore a tsunami had somehow managed to occur on a river. There was no paddling, no steering; we were at the mercy of the water. I must have been the only one on the raft thinking we were going to die because everyone else was laughing and truly enjoying the ride. And then it happened. We were hit by the biggest most powerful wave yet. Even though my vision was totally obscured, I sensed that something was not right - and it wasn't. When my vision returned, the seat immediately in front of me, previously occupied by my daughter, was empty! There she was, on her back about two yards in front of the raft, being rapidly pulled down the river by the current. Being the anal retentive that I am, I began counting - (60, 59, 58 …) and paddling as hard as my arms would let me!

- Are we disciplined enough to remain calm in the face of adversity and enact the plan we carefully laid out?

We closed the gap rather quickly (... 46, 45, 44 ...) but it was then I realized she would be on my side of the raft and I would be the one pulling her in. I had no idea how I could do that and still keep my feet, which I could no longer feel, in the straps and my death grip on the cord attached to the raft. After what seemed like an eternity, but wasn't (... 38, 37 ...) we pulled almost even with her and I knew in a few seconds, when we were ahead of her on the river, I would be required to exercise our rescue plan. But as luck would have it, I did not even have those extra few seconds.

All of a sudden I heard the guide screaming at me to pull her out. How could he be asking me to do that - we weren't in front of her yet?! Did he forget his own plan? When I turned to look at him to see if he was nuts, I saw, or perhaps, sensed it - the reason for his screams. There, standing up in the raft, showing no fear at all, was my wife, paddle held tightly in both hands, wrapped around behind her back in a batting stance that would have made Babe Ruth proud, eyes blazing and a determined look on her face. And then I knew. If I did not pull my daughter out just then - forget the plan - there is no doubt I would have felt the impact of the paddle on my skull and maybe nothing else ever again!

- Do we recognize that everyone reacts differently to stressful situations?

- Do we address the concerns of the individuals and be flexible when things do not go according to plan?

Needless to say, I reacted without thinking, pulling my daughter, who was still laughing hysterically and having a blast, safely on to the raft. It was only then I realized I was unstrapped, held no lifeline and was bouncing around helplessly in the middle of the raft. I quickly remedied that, pulling the foot straps even tighter, if that were even possible, as I sat back in my seat.

- Do we realize how much we can accomplish, in spite of our own limitations, if we have a vision and stay focused on the task, for visions are dreams that execution makes a reality?

Despite the coldness of the water, the heat in the raft from my wife's glares kept us all warm for the rest of the trip.

- Do we recognize that regardless of the outcome, you can't please everyone – that one 'aw s&%t' wipes out all 'atta boys' you have accumulated?

And I had a new appreciation for our guide, who most definitely saved my life that day. There is a lot to say about the value of a Harvard education!

Adaptability

Thoughts on adaptability

- "It is a wise person that adapts themselves to all contingencies; it's the fool who always struggles like a swimmer against the current." - *Anonymous*
- "All living things contain a measure of madness that moves them in strange, sometimes inexplicable ways. This madness can be saving; it is part and parcel of the ability to adapt. Without it, no species would survive." - *Yann Martel, Life of Pi*

Ways leaders are adaptable

- Read, benchmark and learn; be an avid reader
- Multitasks to become comfortable shifting between efforts/ideas
- Keep a holistic view
- Look to others for ideas and suggestions
- Merge ideas to provide best path of action
- Do not start out with a solution or approach; always keep the end in mind
- 'Think outside the box'; be creative; be innovative
- Don't say 'no', say 'how can this work?'
- Focus on changing self (processes/operations) rather than the environment
- Don't judge a book by its cover; don't judge too quickly

Perseverance

[pur-s*uh*-**veer**-*uh* ns]:

...continued effort to do or achieve something despite difficulties, obstacles, discouragement, failure, or opposition

Synonyms: persistence, determination
Antonyms: indecisiveness, tentativeness

Leadership Is...

Perseverance

We can all influence people around us in a positive way, take responsibility to do our best in every situation and work together to build incredible teams. A great example of this happened a few years ago when 8 year old Elizabeth Hughes sang the National Anthem at a minor league hockey game. For any of you who have been to a minor league hockey game, you know how difficult an audience that can be.

Elizabeth was almost at the end of the National Anthem, singing every note on key, perfect pitch, to a quiet audience when her microphone went out and no one could hear her. One would have understood if anyone, much less an 8 year old, 'lost her cool' in a situation like this, but it didn't happen her - not to Elizabeth. She continued on despite the circumstances and in the course of doing so, something special happened. At first, a few near her started to sing with her, being caught up in her determination. But it did not end there; a few moments later the previously muted crowd, *everyone* in the arena, began singing with her - at the top of their lungs, never missing a beat or a note. It was a very touching moment, one that sends a message to all of us.

- Do we create a vision and passion? Leaders, whether formal or informal - by title, role or choice - realize the importance of creating a vision for others to follow. Without it, no one knows what is next or is able to join in.
- Do we 'walk the talk?' Leaders lead by example. They persevere despite the challenges they face. They do not quit!
- Do we generate a passion in others? Leaders inspire, so when they are not there and cannot be heard, others can go on and embrace the initiative enthusiastically and confidently.

Business leaders take great strides in increasing not only the value of their own departments but also in pointing the way for the rest of the company so they, too, can improve. We all need to be leaders. To make that happen, perhaps we can all learn from Elizabeth. If you lead by action, with conviction and confidence-others will step up and follow.

Oh, and did I mention, when Elizabeth finished she was greeted by thunderous applause? True leadership, regardless from whom, is recognized and greatly appreciated.

Perseverance

Thoughts on perseverance

- "With ordinary talents and extraordinary perseverance, all things are attainable." - *Sir Thomas Fowell Buxton*
- "Perseverance is the hard work you do after you get tired of doing the hard work you already did." - *Newt Gingrich*
- "I have not failed. I have just found 10,000 ways that won't work." – *Thomas A. Edison*
- "Most of the important things in the world have been accomplished by people who have kept on trying when there seemed to be no hope at all." - *Dale Carnegie*

Ways leaders persevere

- Challenge and stretch self and others with goals and efforts
- Treat unsuccessful attempts not as failure but as a learning opportunity
- Do not compromise on quality for expediency
- Talk of 'when' not 'if'
- Take breaks from effort if at a stalemate
- Approach solutions one step at a time
- Celebrate small successes
- Use his/her network
- Be a proponent of change, a change manager
- Create 'fun' opportunities during the effort
- Do not let efforts on one project affect approach, attitude or energy in another

Vision

[**vizh**-*uh* n]:

...the act or power of anticipating that which will or may come to be, often under the influence of a divine or other agency

Synonyms: foresight, prophesy
Antonym: shortsighted, thoughtless

Leadership Is…

Vision

I love vacations. I always have. Our family, like many when I was growing up, traveled by car whenever we went on vacation, no matter how far it was. I remember the excitement my brother and I felt, starting days before, even though we knew it meant sitting in the back seat with a huge cooler between us. Our family was frugal but the cramped quarters did nothing to spoil our trip.

Recently, I was reminiscing with a friend. Being of about the same age, his vacation travel as a youth was very similar to mine: always by car and always with a fully stocked cooler with refreshments. The difference was that there were 3 children in his family; he had a brother and a sister. He and his brother, however, were never cramped. Their father had a hatchback; they got to lay down in the back, stretched out and comfortable with an unobstructed view out the large back window, while their sister occupied the back seat with the cooler. Another benefit - that far back the dreaded "Don't make me stop this car!" we all heard on these trips was not as ominous.

It was a perfect way to travel, or so I thought. But his memories of vacation travel were negative, a stark contrast to my happy ones. He hated it! What he remembers is the family, up front, saying things like, "Look at that rock formation!" Or, "Isn't that sunset beautiful?" Or pointing to a billboard, "That would be a great place to go." While he had a majestic panoramic view through the rear window, he was sitting in the back so he had to wait to see the beautiful scenery. Even worse was passing the billboard a minute later never seeing or knowing where it would be great to go, or never getting to see the sunset from his position in the back. For him, facing the rear, even if it was more comfortable, was not enjoyable.

Thinking about our different perspectives during basically the same experiences makes me wonder about our journey.

- Do we realize that the journey may be more important than the destination?
- Do we as a leader make our employees comfortable which may lead to complacency?
- Do we excite and challenge them by allowing everyone to be forward-looking, asking them to foresee the future rather than view the past?

The same holds true for each of us as individuals; are we comfortable or challenged? Comfort is nice, but it will not bring about the same opportunities for growth we all need to succeed. We need to step out of our comfort zone to know what we can really accomplish. We need to dream, to see the possibilities, and strive for them.

Remember, you can't win one of my favorite car ride games – 'I Spy' – by looking out the rear window!

Vision

Thoughts on vision

- "The most pathetic person in the world is someone who has sight, but has no vision." - *Helen Keller*
- "I can teach anybody how to get what they want out of life. The problem is that I can't find anybody who can tell me what they want." - *Mark Twain*
- "Where there is no vision the people perish." - *Proverbs 29:18*

Ways a leader instills vision

- Talk to others to understand their dreams and aspirations
- Define personal and company values and communicate them to others
- Look long term; predict future needs and conditions
- Be comprehensive; include who will be served, what will be provided, how will it provided
- Include others in the development process
- Be optimistic; incorporate a goal/vision that is a stretch well above where you and the competition are today but realistic
- Constantly communicate progress
- Align all organizations and identify their role and responsibility in the attainment of the vision
- Make the vision simple, specific yet general; provide the direction and end goal but allow employees the ability to envision it as they see it

Positive Expectations

[**poz**-i-tiv ek-spek-**tey**-sh*uh* nz]:

...a feeling or belief about how successful, good, etc., someone or something can be

Synonyms: optimism, confidence
Antonyms: negativity, uncertainty

Leadership Is...

Positive Expectations

Dinner was over. Mom was in the kitchen cleaning up, appreciating the few minutes of relative peace and quiet. She was taking advantage of time away from her two boys, nine and eleven. It seems they were always into everything; many of her friends said they were just boys being boys, but they didn't have to live with these two, she thought.

As she was finishing up the dishes, her husband came in and asked how her day went - so she told him. She started with the boys turning the clocks back so they could sleep later and miss the bus *causing her to have to drive them to school.* Then the detention they got for gluing the teacher's pens, papers, and paperclips to the desk *causing her to have to pick them up as well.* And finally and most emphatically about them spray painting their cat pink after school.

For the boys, this was an easy day, one that was gradually becoming normal. For Mom, however, she had reached the end of her rope; it was more than she could handle.

Now these were good parents who encouraged their children to learn, grow, and have fun. They tried to teach and impose acceptable rules to make the boys behave better, but they were too often disappointed. They had come to expect the worst, and that is what they received. At their wit's end, they were desperately seeking a solution.

The father told his wife about a Priest at a near-by Church. He had heard from a friend that this Priest worked with youth and apparently had great success in helping them find their way. She was ready for anything, so he called and made an appointment for the boys to meet with the Priest on Saturday.

The weekend came, and after introductions and some polite chit-chat, the Priest told the parents they could go home, which was only a few blocks away. He would call when they were done.

When they left, the Priest sat the boys across the table from him and asked the younger one in a quiet and fatherly voice, "Where is God?"

The boy just looked at him in silence, so the Priest decided to use a slightly more pious voice, once again asking the young man, "Where is God?" Noticing the more secular, official voice, the boy squirmed a little in his seat but still did not say a word.

Sensing he needed to step it up a notch, the Priest went into his office, put on his robes and returned to face the boy again. This time, standing in front of the boy, using the voice he used for delivering sermons, he waved his finger in the boy's face and boomed, "Where is God!?"

With this, the boy's eyes widened and he bolted from the chair, followed closely by his brother. They ran straight home, rushing through the front door, past their parents, and into their room. The parents immediately went to the boys' room to see what happened, only to find them cowering in their closet. They asked their sons, "What's the matter?"

The boys, trembling, answered, "God is missing and they think we had something to do with it!"

- Do we sometimes label people and consequently set expectations that become self-full filling prophecies?

- Do we stereotype people so we don't give them a chance or, maybe more importantly, don't allow them to give themselves a chance?

- Do we recognize the value of having everyone on the team with the same vision, pulling in the same direction?

Expectations too often become self-fulfilling prophesies, so leaders set expectations high, for themselves and for others. They understand the ability of those in whom you believe to accomplish what you dream for them. They know that whether you think you will fail or succeed - you will be right!

It all starts with what you believe. Believe in the good in yourself and others.

Positive Expectations

Thoughts on positive expectations

- "Don't blame people for disappointing you, blame yourself for expecting too much from them." - *Anonymous*
- "What screws us up the most in life is the picture in our heads of how it's supposed to be." – *Anonymous*
- "Dream more than others think practical...Expect more than others think possible." - *Howard Schultz, Starbucks Coffee*

Ways leaders set positive expectations

- Set positive goals and remain optimistic
- Communicate the benefits
- Praise proper behavior
- Coach when performance slacks
- Involve others in goal setting
- Encourage new projects, new efforts and educate
- Allow employees to pursue their passion
- Celebrate even small successes
- Do not belittle or criticize
- Share and communicate the vision of others

Prioritization

[prahy-**awr**-i-tez-a- shun]:

...the listing or rating of items based on their relative importance, presumably to ensure the most important items are addressed first

Synonyms: ordering, ranking
Antonyms: chaos, disarray

Leadership Is...

Prioritization

It was finally time for the long anticipated weekend getaway. Four young women just starting their professional careers, had planned this weekend in the mountains for months. They'd talked to their bosses and all had managed to leave work at 3:00 pm so they could get to their cabin in time to enjoy a nice dinner after the anticipated four and a half hour drive.

The trip started out as you would expect. Conversation went on non-stop from the moment they entered the car, covering topics from boys to clothes, from gossip to the economy, and everything in between - with much of it going on simultaneously. It was the beginning of what was to be the ideal weekend.

The scenery was beautiful as they wound their way up the narrow roads of the mountain. Night fell about an hour before they were to arrive at their destination, but that did nothing to dampen their spirits. About thirty minutes from their destination they were startled as they rounded a curve and came upon a police car on the side of the road with its lights flashing. As they slowed to pass they noticed the young patrolman standing in front of the vehicle, looking exceptionally pale in the headlights. When they asked if he was okay, his fear was evident as he said in a low voice, as if speaking to no one at all, "The van just drove straight off the cliff," all the while staring down into the ravine below. When the women looked down to where the officer was pointing they saw a van that had obviously rolled down the cliff and was now resting on the driver's side of the car.

Without a moment's hesitation, my daughter, Lauren, and her friend, Leslie, said, "We're nurses. Can we help?" The look of desperation on the officer's face turned into one of relief as he hollered, "Please!" So Lauren and Leslie jumped out of the car and slid down the 40 foot ravine to the car below. A family of 5 was inside: the father and the teenage daughter were unconscious; the mother was bleeding profusely from a cut on her head; the youngest son, about 6 years old, was in shock; and the older brother was dazed and bleeding but coherent. It was obvious that the accident had just occurred.

After checking on everyone's condition and tending to the immediate needs, the women determined it was okay to move them; they climbed back up the ravine, the first time to get the blankets and towels they had brought for their trip to create a pallet for the family to rest on, followed immediately by another trip to get the jackets and sweatshirts to keep them warm in the cool mountain air. When the women had the family out of the vehicle and as comfortable as possible, they were better able to treat the injuries they could with the limited supplies available. When the ambulance arrived, they had already triaged the victims, and after alerting the EMTs to each person's condition, they made the long, slow climb back out of the ravine.

They finally finished the trip to the cabin, arriving two hours late, a lot dirtier than expected, and with significantly fewer supplies than they set out with, leaving the blankets and clothes behind for the victims. No one ever asked, nor did they ever think of, telling them their names.

- How good are we at recognizing when someone is in need of help at work? Do we take the time to question and look for 'signs' beyond the obvious or is our goal to just make our day as stress free and easy as possible?

- Do we offer help unquestioningly and quickly?

- Do we require recognition for ourselves before we will reach out a hand?

- When we are faced with multiple priorities, are we able 'triage' them and address the most important ones first?

Lauren came home with a cold from that trip because of the time spent in the cool air helping that family and a weekend without a jacket and blanket, but she had a wonderful time. She says it was because she was with her friends but I can't help but wonder if her selfless act didn't have a little to do with it as well.

Prioritization

Thoughts on prioritization

- "We must keep the main thing the main thing." – *Jim Barksdale*
- "The key is not to prioritize what's on your schedule, but to schedule your priorities." - *Stephen Covey*

Ways a leader prioritizes

- Understand 'mission-critical' versus 'want (or nice) to haves'
- Think through issues before acting; take the time to plan
- Manage time effectively; schedule time for personal, e-mail, etc.
- Do not say 'yes' to everything; turn down projects if not essential
- Set clear goals and objectives
- Use a matrix (e.g.: benefit, cost, skills available, time to completion, probability of implementation, options available) to decide
- Do not mistake action for results
- Be innovative; look for alternatives
- Do not procrastinate; decide and act quickly
- Eliminate bias; seek and take advice from others

Trust

[truhst]:

...belief that someone or something is reliable, good, honest, effective, etc., generating the confidence of a (favorable) outcome of a future event

Synonyms: belief, faith
Antonyms: doubt, suspicion

Leadership Is...

Trust

There was a woman, Arial, who loved the circus. It started when she was 5, when her parents took her to the circus for her birthday. The clowns, the elephants, the lions, the trapeze were exciting - but her true love was the tightrope walker. The required precision, being so far above the ground, the gasps from the crowd, all mesmerized her. For the next several years Arial went to the circus every time it was in town and waited for the act she loved!

But time went on, as it does. Arial grew up, went to school, got a job, got married and moved to a small town. Other commitments and priorities took the place of the circus. Two years after getting married, Arial and her husband had a little girl. They were overjoyed and loved their daughter dearly. A few years later, a circus came to town, and as you would expect, Arial could not wait to share this experience with her daughter. She took the entire family to opening night and was once again enamored by the tightrope walker.

- Do we allow people to lose their passion because of other priorities?

Her husband noticed Arial's infatuation with the act and asked her about it when they arrived home. To his surprise, she told him about her love of the act, her passion for tightrope walking and, before she knew it, and not even realizing it was true, blurted out that she really wanted to learn how to do it. Instead of the laughter she expected, her husband understood and encouraged her to do so. Together they laid out the plan to make her dream a reality.

- Do we encourage others to pursue their passion, regardless of the obstacles?

They started slowly. Arial learned by walking on a 2x4 board lying on the ground. Later, the board was turned on its side, narrow edge up, still at ground level. After a few days the board was raised - a little each day, until it was about 4 feet off the ground. They then progressively narrowed the width of the walking surface - first to thinner boards, then to a thick and eventually to a narrow rope. During the process, a long pole was added to assist with Arial's balance. This gradual, thoughtful approach to learning how to walk the tightrope went on for months, with her husband by her side providing encouragement every step of the way. Finally Arial was walking the tightrope over 20 feet in the air, loving every minute of it!

- Do we create a safe environment, with proper tools and resources, for continuous learning?

On her birthday, Arial's husband told her how proud he was of her and, for a special treat, had arranged for her to walk the tightrope at the circus when it came to town a few months later. She was excited and terrified. She was torn between the fear of embarrassment and the thrill of accomplishment, but she finally did accept.

- Do we set high goals for ourselves and others?

- Do we provide the opportunity for others to be a 'star?'

Arial accepted, but she wanted her debut to be memorable, something her daughter could be proud of. So she came up with the idea of walking the tightrope pushing a wheelbarrow. Despite her husband's initial shock, he agreed to help her, so the lessons began again, this time each step was performed and practiced with the wheelbarrow.

The time was finally here; the circus was in town and Arial was ready. As she and her husband stood in the wings waiting for her to be announced, she had second thoughts and was thinking of not going through with it! Her husband knew she was ready and told her so. Still, she was fearful; he told her of his confidence in her and her ability to succeed. Her trepidation subsided, but was not yet eliminated. As the music introducing her act began her husband, knowing the danger of performing with doubts, asked what he could do to make her understand he had complete trust in her ability - he knew she would succeed.

Then, after a few seconds of silence, he saw her begin to relax, begin to smile slightly; she looked him in the eye and said, "Get in the wheelbarrow."

- Are we willing to put our full trust in our employees, putting our fate in their hands?

If we have done our job right, developing employees with a well-thought out plan, providing appropriate resources, exhibiting encouragement and patience, and creating an environment in which they can safely take risks, then it is truly time for us to get in the wheelbarrow!

Trust

Thoughts on trust

- "Trust each other again and again. When the trust level gets high enough, people transcend apparent limits, discovering new and awesome abilities for which they were previously unaware." -*David Armistead*
- "...there are no mistakes, only lessons. Love yourself, trust your choices, and everything is possible." *Cheri Carter Scotts*
- "eBay's business is based on enabling someone to do business with another person, and to do that, they first have to develop some measure of trust, either in the other person or the system." - *Pierre Omidyar*

Ways leaders build trust

- Do not talk badly of others
- Say what he means and does what he says
- Follow through on all commitments
- Be proactive in keeping all informed
- Keep 'secrets' and confidences
- Act on values consistently
- Stand up for employees as required
- Stay organized; document everything; keep promises
- Be politically correct, yet honest
- Have no underlying agenda
- Do not exaggerate
- Get results, achieve objectives/promises/commitments

Respect

[ri-**spekt**]:

...a feeling or understanding that someone or something Is important, serious, etc., and should be treated in an appropriate way

Synonyms: admiration, esteem
Antonyms: contempt, disregard

Leadership Is...

Respect

My wife's Uncle Tuck, died recently; Gayle, my wife, was the child he never had, so they were very close. Tuck was a good man; he was a proud veteran of World War II; he was a loving husband who was faithfully married for over 60 years; he was a loyal employee who held his job at the government depot for almost 35 years before retiring; he was a religious man who never uttered a curse word or a bad word about anyone, at least not until he suffered from severe Alzheimer's almost 5 years ago. That is when he got so violent he had to be put on medication that took away his quality of life and made all conversation and interaction with him impossible.

During the visitation, service and funeral, I was impressed by a number of things. First, there were a lot of people at the funeral home, service and gravesite. Now Tuck was 89 years old, so I was somewhat surprised by the turnout. Only a few of his friends were there; I expected this, for most of them had already passed away. There was family; but with no children and only 1 brother, that circle was not large either.

The majority of those in attendance were strangers - neighbors, church members and towns' people - most of whom had not seen him in years. Looking at how young many of those people were, the chances were they never had met Tuck at all; they knew about him only through their parents. It struck me how great a tribute it was for him to have these people, who had only known *of* him and what he stood for, to take the time to honor him in this way.

After the service, the procession of vehicles from the Church to the cemetery took almost 30 minutes, traversing through the city streets of Collierville, Tennessee, and through the country roads leading to Independence, Mississippi. Along the way, I was amazed to see cars that were traveling in the opposite direction pull over to the side of the road and stop, waiting for the entire procession to go by before resuming their journey, even though they would not have impeded our progress had they kept going. I was even more amazed to see joggers and people walking their dogs stop at the sight of the procession, take their hats off and stand still as we passed by.

When we got to the final large intersection prior to reaching the cemetery, every member of the police escort was off his motorcycle, standing in the road as we drove by. The younger ones, the non-veterans, had their hands over their hearts; the older ones, those that had served in the military, were in full salute. All were standing as if they were statues, staring straight ahead, not moving a muscle, until every last car had passed. Not one of them knew this man whom we called Tuck.

Now Tuck was not a famous man; he did not do anything I am aware of that would draw local, much less national, attention, but I cannot help but think how blessed I am to have known him. Those who attended the funeral must have felt the same way. They remembered the real Tuck and what he did throughout his life; not what he had become these last few years.

- Have we created a legacy for ourselves, personally and professionally that will be remembered despite what happens to us from here on?

- Do we realize that our actions establish our reputation, a reputation that touches far more than just those with whom we interact directly in life?

- Is the legacy we have established the reputation by which we want to be remembered?

The entire experience brought tears to my eyes. Many of those tears were brought on by the actions of strangers - removing their hats, stopping their cars, saluting in silence, attending the ceremonies - all for someone they may never have met, but to whom it did not matter; for while they may never have met him, through his actions they most certainly knew him.

- Do we provide everyone, those we know and those we don't know, those we like and those we don't like, with the respect and honor they deserve? It is an indication of who you are. At work, it creates an environment of respect that will foster cooperation and results.

Tuck, you showed me, by example, the way to live, and even in death, you taught me additional lessons which I will always cherish. Thank you; you will be missed but not forgotten.

Respect

Thoughts on respect

- "If you have some respect for people as they are, you can be more effective in helping them to become better than they are." - *John W. Gardner*
- "Respect...is appreciation of the separateness of the other person, of the ways in which he or she is unique." - *Annie Gottlieb*
- "Respect is earned, not given; respect is provisional, not perpetual." – *Bob Bennett*

Ways leaders instill respect

- 'Walk the talk'; be a role model
- Strive to do your best on any task, large or small
- Be true to your word
- See and consider the views of others
- Resolve issues quickly and directly with the party(ies) involved; do not speak poorly of others
- Speak the truth, not rumors or conjecture; be sincere
- Stand up for your values and beliefs
- Dress and act appropriately; respect yourself
- Speak confidently
- Go out of your way to help
- Remember your manners

Reputation

[rep-y*uh*-**tey**-sh*uh* n]:

...the common opinion that people have about someone or something

Synonyms: status, character
Antonyms: disgrace, unprincipled

Leadership Is...

Reputation

Yes, Virginia, there is a Santa Claus! You may have heard this before - it was the beginning of an unsigned editorial in The New York Sun on September 21, 1897, in response to a letter received from eight-year-old Virginia O'Hanlon asking if there really was a Santa Claus. Her friends told her he did not exist providing plausible reasons: there was no way Santa could travel around the world in one night; reindeer don't fly; he is too fat to get down the chimney. But Virginia saw the evidence - all the presents under her tree every Christmas; the cookies eaten; the milk drunk. Could she be wrong? She saw it herself! She wanted to know - she did not want to be embarrassed.

That is something I can relate to for I, as I leave the house each day I can still hear my mother asking, "Did you comb your hair?", and my wife, years later saying "You're not going to wear *that*, are you?" While not feeling the love at the time, I realize now that they were all meant, at least in part, to save me from embarrassment - the same thing Virginia was trying to avoid.

With many of us traveling for the holidays to share joy and happiness with friends and family, I thought it would be a good time to share an airport 'seeing is believing' story my friend, Jorge, recently shared with me. This is another that you may have heard previously, but the leadership lesson is important enough to be repeated.

Jorge was traveling on a flight from Seattle to San Francisco. Since he travels frequently, and like most of us cannot afford first class, he booked a seat at the bulk-head. The bulk head, for those that may not know, is the first row of seats behind the curtain that separates First Class from Coach. Jorge did this to get the extra leg room it provided.

Shortly after getting settled, he noticed the pilot, a tall, dark haired gentleman wearing his aviation sunglasses, yes, even though he was inside the plane!

The pilot was helping a woman and her seeing-eye dog to the seat across the aisle from Jorge. The woman took this flight often, for it was obvious that she and the pilot knew each other well. After putting her luggage overhead for her and getting her and her dog settled in the front row of coach (the seats next to her went unfilled, presumably to accommodate her dog), the pilot thanked her for flying with them again and turned her over to the flight attendant with specific orders to take care of her every need.

- Do we value the importance of personalized customer service and understand its impact on our company and personal brand/reputation?

Take-off was smooth, but shortly thereafter, as luck would have it, the flight was unexpectedly diverted to Sacramento due to weather. The flight attendant explained apologetically that there would be a slight delay and informed the passengers that they were more than welcome to get off the aircraft and stretch their legs if they desired. A large number of people got off but Jorge and the blind woman remained on board.

Soon after, the pilot got up to stretch his legs and noticed the woman still seated. He walked back to her seat, touched her gently on the shoulder as he called her by name and said, "Flora, we are going to be here for about an hour. Are you sure you don't want to get up and move around? I will be more than happy to come and bring you back on before we resume the flight."

The woman was most appreciative, but she hesitated in her reply, finally telling the pilot, "No thank you. I don't need to, but I wonder if I should so Archie (which turned out to be her dog) can walk around a little. He must be so cramped in this small space." The pilot immediately volunteered to take her dog for a walk in the concourse if she did not wish to go. She quickly agreed, being so grateful that Jorge could hear the happiness in her voice. The pilot leaned over, picked up the dog's lead, and walked him off the airplane for her.

- Do we 'go the extra mile' for our customers, family and friends with no thought for ourselves?

As the pilot and Archie stepped off the jet way leading from the plane to the terminal area, everyone in the vicinity stopped and stared.

After a few moments of silence, a frantic scramble occurred as passengers ran to the nearest staffed airline counters to change or cancel their reservations. They all formed the same perception/conclusion - that the airline must have lenient policies toward hiring for diversity!

For all they saw was a pilot walking off a plane, being led by a guide dog and yes, he was still wearing his dark aviator sunglasses!

Perceptions do become reality if people are not informed, and first impressions are hard to change. That is why one of my first bosses would always say, Don't ever give even the slightest hint of impropriety. Make sure your appearance, behavior, and actions portray how you want to be known, for that is how you will be remembered as well. Seeing is believing.

Reputation

Thoughts on reputation

- "It takes 20 years to build a reputation and five minutes to ruin it. If you think about that, you'll do things differently."
  - Warren Buffett
- "You can't build a reputation on what you are going to do."
  - Henry Ford

Ways leaders establish reputation

- Make others 'look good'
- Offer opinions and thoughts honestly but tactfully
- Take on new responsibilities without being asked
- Do not let personal bias (or friendships) get in the way of doing the right thing
- Provide meaningful results; exceed expectations
- Go 'out of your way' to help
- Network; cultivate respected associates
- Support local community causes
- Be visible at all levels
- Participate in industry organizations; take on leadership roles
- Speak at events and to media (with training) when possible
- Take responsibility when appropriate
- Be fair; treat others with respect

Integrity

[in-**teg**-ri-tee]:

...the quality of being honest and fair

Synonyms: honesty, honor, reliability
Antonyms: dishonesty, deceit, corruption

Leadership Is...

Integrity

Integrity may mean different things to different people - the most common having to do with being honest and telling the truth. But I think there is another aspect of integrity that is just as important, and one that can clearly and only be shown through actions over time.

Years ago, we lived next door to a family of 5: a Mom and Dad and their three children. My girls became best friends with their children and they were inseparable. They were always together, laughing and playing. As such, it was important for me to be assured that the values we held dear for our children were also important for their friends. It was what happened during an unhappy time that made me feel more comfortable that they had, in fact, chosen the right friends.

Our neighbors' Labrador retriever, whom they had for over 14 years, died one evening. Their children, who were relatively young, were devastated. They insisted on having the dog buried in their back yard. The father told them it was too late to perform a burial that night, but he promised they would bury their beloved pet the next morning. That night, he cleaned out his freezer chest, bringing some of his food to our place for temporary storage, so they could put the dog, wrapped appropriately in a tarp, in it to keep until the next morning. He then went out and dug the grave for the dog, thinking this would make it easier for all of them the next day. They woke up the next morning to a torrential downpour; the funeral was delayed as the parents waited, hoped and prayed for a break in the weather.

But the children were crying endlessly. The rain continued and the forecast indicated there was no hope of the rain letting up any time soon. The father knew a decision had to be made quickly.

I couldn't help but smile as I looked out my window that day; the smile was, in part, because I recognized the important lesson he was teaching his children. Yet I have to admit, most of the smile was due to the scene below. There he was, in the pouring rain, with an umbrella in one hand and a Bible in the other, conducting the service with one foot outstretched, trying to push a frozen, *floating* dog into a grave that had filled with water.

Eventually the ceremony was completed and the grave was covered. The children were happy - because what mattered most to them was not how smoothly the burial went, but that they got to bury the family pet in the yard. And the father made that happen.

- Do we fulfill our commitments to our employees and customers, in spite of the obstacles that arise?

- Do we yield to the pressures of 'now,' failing to recognize the value of trust and integrity for the long term?

Integrity

Thoughts on integrity

- "Real integrity is doing the right thing, knowing that nobody's going to know whether you did it or not." - *Oprah Winfrey*
- "Integrity is not a conditional word. It doesn't blow in the wind or change with the weather. It is your inner image of yourself, and if you look in there and see a man who won't cheat, then you know he never will." - *John D. MacDonald*
- "In looking for people to hire, you look for three qualities: integrity, intelligence, and energy. And if they don't have the first, the other two will kill you." - *Warren Buffet*
- "Trust is a result of your actions and a reflection of who you really are." – *Bob Bennett*

Ways leaders show integrity

- Clearly define your values and principles
- Determine your behaviors that will achieve these values
- Be honest with yourself; know your strengths and weaknesses
- Do not allow biases to affect decisions and actions
- Speak the truth
- Accept and appreciate the opinions of others
- Have a mentor or 'trusted counsel'
- Consider the 'whole rather than the moment'; put others first
- Surround yourself with others of integrity

Utilization

[**yoot**-l-ah – za- shuh n]:

...the use of something for a particular purpose

Synonyms: application, deployment
Antonyms: doing without, relinquishing

Leadership Is...

Utilization

This is an old tale from the Middle East that a friend of mine passed along to me. He felt, and rightfully so, that while we may have heard it before the message bears repeating.

A water bearer in Pakistan had two large pots, each hung on the end of a pole which he carried across his neck. One of the pots had a crack in it, and while the other pot was perfect and always delivered a full portion of water at the end of the long walk from the stream to the master's house, the cracked pot arrived only half full.

For a full 2 years this went on daily, with the bearer delivering only one and a half pots full of water to his master's house. Of course, the perfect pot was proud of its accomplishments, perfect for the job for which it was made. But the poor cracked pot was ashamed of its own imperfection, and miserable that it was able to accomplish only half of what it had been made to do. After 2 years of what it perceived to be bitter failure, it spoke to the water bearer one day by the stream.

"I am ashamed of myself, and I want to apologize to you."

"Why?" asked the bearer. "What are you ashamed of?"

"I have been able, for these past two years, to deliver only half my load because this crack in my side causes water to leak out all the way back to your master's house. Because of my flaws, you have to do all of this work, and you don't get full value from your efforts," the pot said.

The water bearer felt sorry for the old cracked pot, and in his compassion he said, "As we return to the master's house, I want you to notice the beautiful flowers along the path."

Indeed as they went up the hill, the old cracked pot took notice of the sun warming the beautiful wild flowers on the side of the path and this cheered it some. But at the end of the trail, it still felt bad because it had leaked out half its load, and so again it apologized to the bearer for its failure.

The bearer said to the pot, "Did you notice that there were flowers only on *your* side of your path, but not on the other pot's side? That's because I have always known about your flaw, and I took advantage of it. I planted flower seeds on your side of the path, and every day while we walk back from the stream, you've watered them. For 2 years I have been able to pick these beautiful flowers to decorate my master's table. Without you being just the way you are, he would not have this beauty to grace his house."

Each of us has our own unique flaws. We're all 'cracked pots.' It is the cracks and flaws we each have that make us unique, that allows us to do things that others cannot. It is these differences that make our lives together so very interesting and rewarding.

- Do we look for the strengths in others or do we focus solely on their 'flaws'/weaknesses?
- Do we utilize the strengths of each individual appropriately or do we try to force them into the 'box' we create for them?
- Do we maximize the value of the abilities/skills we possess and of others – do we not waste the talent with which we are blessed?

We must accept each person for who they are and look for the good in them. We need to develop that good, let it grow and use it appropriately. We should be especially grateful for those who are flexible, for they shall not be bent out of shape.

Appreciate all people in your life! If it wasn't for the crackpots, our life would be pretty boring!

Utilization

Thoughts on utilization

- "Get the right people on the bus and in the right seat." - *Jim Collins*
- "Be wise in the use of time. The question in life is not 'how much time do we have?' The question is 'what shall we do with it?'" – *Anna Robertson Brown*
- "Success is the maximum utilization of the ability that you have." - *Zig Ziglar*

Ways leaders improve utilization

- Allow people to follow their passion
- Cross-train employees
- Ensure objectives and vision are well known
- Promote teamwork through joint efforts
- Be available
- Coach and encourage
- Be innovative; stay current with advancements in technology and processes
- Benchmark often
- Plan in detail
- Use metrics to monitor progress
- Get feedback from team and customers regularly
- Be receptive to ideas from others (especially users)
- Be flexible; change direction or actions when or as needed

Responsibility

[ri-spon-s*uh*-**bil**-i-tee]:

...the state of being the person who caused something (usually a duty or task you are required or expected to do) to happen

Synonyms: duty, accountability
Antonyms: carelessness, negligence

Leadership Is...

Responsibility

It was just one of those days. You know what I mean. We all have them. No matter what you do, nothing seems to go right.

A good friend and FedEx colleague had a day like that a few years back. It didn't start like many of them do, with a sleepless night, tossing and turning, worrying about a presentation to be given in front of hundreds of people, or how to tell your boss bad news, or how to deal with a troubled employee. No, the night's sleep went fine; as a matter of fact, it went too well. Julie slept like a baby. So much so that when she did awake, she saw the light streaming in through the sides of the blinds. Knowing that this was not normal, she immediately sat up in bed and turned to the electric clock on her nightstand. Sure enough, she had overslept by 45 minutes. Her clock apparently had not gone off due to a power outage that occurred sometime during the night.

- Do we remember the value of contingency plans, even for the simplest and most ordinary events?

Jumping out of bed, all she could think of was that she was conducting interviews that morning for a critical position within her organization. She was stressed, for who would want to work for someone who couldn't even be on time for her own meeting?! Julie was on a mission: a run through the shower while brushing her teeth; pulling her hair back into a pony-tail rather than putting it up as usual; sliding a dress over her head as she stepped into the first pair of shoes she could find. As she headed for the door in such a rush she was proud of how quickly she got out of the house, even if the shower was still dripping, the bathroom floor was soaked and littered with pajamas and towels, and the countertop and sink contained slowly hardening toothpaste blobs.

Pulling out of the driveway she heard the incessant ding - ding from her car. Alright, alright, she thought, I will put on my seat belt. But as she drove off after buckling in, she was surprised the sound continued. Looking down, she saw that the sound was to alert her of low fuel - she had an 18 mile ride to work and a gauge that said 8 miles to empty! Julie headed straight to the nearest gas station, and as luck would have it, found a line of cars waiting their turn. With no choice but to wait, she sat there rather impatiently thinking, 'What else could go wrong?'

After a few minutes (which seemed like hours) she pulled up to the pump, only to find a sign that said the credit card reader did not work. A quick run to the manned booth and back left her a little breathless as she put the hose in the tank. While filling up, a smile began to appear on her lips, the first of the day, as she thought of her skirt and blouse, a new purchase she was wearing for the first time. Looking down at her outfit, the smile vanished quickly as she realized her shoes did not match. Oh, they matched the outfit well – they just did not match each other! "Oh well, I can sit behind the desk all day and maybe no one will notice," she thought. Pulling the nozzle from the tank, she spilled gas on her car, but with no time to clean it up she prayed for rain to wash it off before it faded the paint.

- Are we disciplined enough not to sweat the small stuff?

- Do we do things right the first time, even when time may be pressing?

As Julie pulled out of the gas station, she cut off another car speeding along in the right hand lane doing at least double the speed limit. The driver of the black Chevy, a blonde woman in her 30s, leaned on and did not take her hand off the horn for far longer than she needed to. Julie waved her hand in apology, even though she knew, had the other driver been observing the speed limit this would never have happened. The woman driver responded by tail-gating her for the next mile or two, clearly demonstrating her dissatisfaction with what had just occurred. Looking in the rear view mirror, Julie could see the woman's arms flailing and lips moving, forming words that surely were commenting on Julie, her family and her ancestry. Just as Julie thought she had enough, the woman shot into the left lane, sped by her, only slowing down enough to give Julie the universal one finger salute with her right hand.

- Do we recognize how our moods and actions can affect those around us?

Arriving at the office with 15 minutes to spare, Julie rushed to get the room set up and the questions ready as she tried to relax from the tensions of the morning. The last thing she wanted was to lose the right candidate because of her mood.

Finally ready, with coffee in hand and seated at the conference room table, Julie called in her first interviewee. The most striking thing she saw when the candidate walked in was the coiffed, bright yellow hair on this young woman. Julie rose and extended her hand to introduce herself (while staying behind the table to hide her shoes.) There was a slight pause; perhaps it was the red flush that quickly passed over the woman's face, but it was only a moment before Julie recognized the woman who, not more than 30 minutes ago, had 'honored' her with the 'You're Number 1' sign as she drove by. A smile began to form on Julie's face as her day got a little brighter!

- Do we allow the moods and actions of others to affect the way act and who we are?

You are responsible for your moods, feelings and actions. Make sure they are consistent with who you are and how you want to be regarded/remembered. The ability to maintain control under trying circumstances distinguishes a leader and brings out the best in others as well.

Responsibility

Thoughts on responsibility

- "The price of greatness is responsibility." – *Sir Winston Churchill*
- "Nothing is unconditional – trust, faith, engagement, not even love. Even if it were, it is not free. There is always an expectation attached. It is that expectation that is the basis of and generates responsibility." – *revision of statement from Katja Millay*

Ways leaders promote responsibility

- Make hard decisions; do not be afraid to 'be alone'
- Settle differences and disagreements quickly and effectively; usually 1:1
- Be visible and lead
- Champion ideas, even unpopular ones if they are of value
- 'Suffer the slings and arrows' of critics professionally with courage
- Sell ideas throughout all levels of the organization
- Use his/her network to achieve results
- Build support one person at a time
- 'Push the envelope'; do not become paralyzed by fear or challenges
- Admit when you are wrong
- Remain calm and in control

Compassion

[k*uh* m-**pash**-*uh* n]:

...a sympathetic consciousness of others' distress together with a desire to alleviate it, i.e., a feeling of wanting to help someone who is sick, hungry, in trouble, etc.

Synonyms: concern, kindness, caring
Antonyms: coldness, callousness

Leadership Is...

Compassion

"Hi, my name is Bob and I am ..." I have a confession to make, but I am sure that I am not alone.

We have all experienced *them* and even scarier is that many of us will become one, if not during our normal career, possibly in retirement.

I am talking about consultants. They do a great job of *greasing the wheels* to make things go smoothly, to happen in the way that it is intended. But in spite of this, I have yet to find anyone who embraces them or dreams of growing up to be one. Come to think of it, I am not even sure I know anyone who has ever claimed to have a consultant as a close friend. I wonder if that is because consultants don't advertise their profession, and who can blame them since they are often seen as someone who has no knowledge of what is going on and who only parrots back what employees tell them. And that is their value:

- Do we listen closely to our employees to better understand what is important or do we hire someone to listen for us?

This story is not about consultants per se, but rather about a small, relatively new company which manufactured and sold automobile parts. When it first went into business, its commitment to the customer and its quality product allowed it to gather a profitable, albeit a very small, niche. After about a year, however, costs began to rise steadily and customers were leaving at a pace that would drive them out of business in a relatively short time.

Something had to be done so they hired an independent consultant to help them enhance the productivity of their one and only manufacturing plant. It didn't take long for the consultant to identify the problem. The company was small and operating with limited equipment. To increase profits, management made the decision to continually increase the hours of operation of its one and only plant until it was running 24 hours a day, 7 days a week. At first, this allowed them to keep up with their growing demand. But now they were operating 24/7, and were unable to keep up with what had recently turned into a continually declining demand.

Machine failures were on the rise and quality failures increased as products rolled off the assembly line out of specification. This resulted in temporary shut-downs and, consequently, lost production time. A significant number of delivered products were returned as defective, causing customer dissatisfaction. When products could not be delivered as promised, revenue decreased as a result of lost sales. The lower revenue and rising costs had virtually eliminated any prospect of achieving a favorable profit margin.

Worse yet, they were experiencing higher turnover. More employees had idle time and rework time. They were growing weary of the longer hours; they were no longer proud of the product and, consequently, of the company for which they worked; they did not have any hope of conditions improving any time soon.

- Do we recognize that every decision made has an impact, on our employees?

Fortunately the solution was relatively simple: shut down the machinery for an hour every week to perform routine maintenance on the equipment. The results: an improved product quality, virtually no lost/down time, and almost zero returns. Customers returned, volume grew, revenue increased and yields exceeded previous levels. Profitability – and employee satisfaction - returned.

- Can we look at the business holistically and avoid the 'ready, fire, aim' reaction caused by a narrow focus?

We all experience pressure to produce more with better quality. It is essential in this rapidly challenging world. But we can't become so consumed with one thought, with one part of the operation that we forget it is not a business that produces, but rather its people.

- Do we *schedule maintenance* for ourselves and our teams as well as for our equipment?
- Have we created an environment that will produce more over the *long haul* than what is attainable by just working harder?

A successful business sits upon a three-legged stool of people, service and profit. Keeping them in balance is critical. The leg most often overlooked is the people; be sure they get their scheduled maintenance through mandatory vacations and breaks – it will provide significant benefit, for, if nothing else, it should make it unnecessary for you to hire a consultant.

Compassion

Thoughts on compassion

- "But if we have … compassion and … kindness in us, the people around us will be influenced by our way of being and living." - *Thich Nhat Hanh*
- "When morality comes up against profit, it is seldom that profit loses." - *Shirley Chisholm*
- "He who feels no compassion will become insane." - *Hasidic Saying*

Ways leaders show compassion

- Empathize with others; do not let it turn into sympathy
- Treat each issue as if it was happening to you
- Do not let emotions determine appropriate actions
- Understand the ultimate goals to be achieved and the impact variations from policy may cause
- Keep the 'common good' in mind, but deal with each issue individually
- Create an environment that encourages sharing
- Establish a culture of teamwork and compassion within the workgroup
- Listen carefully; do not be judgmental
- Share your own experiences but keep the focus on others
- Offer help; find options to overcome difficulties
- Provide comfort; physical contact has been proven to be highly effective (e.g., touching someone's hand); exercise it where/when/how/if appropriate

Commitment

[k*uh*-**mit**-m*uh* nt]:

...the attitude of someone who works very hard to do or support something, usually accompanied by the state or an instance of being obligated or emotionally impelled

Synonyms: devotion, obligation
Antonyms: indifference, unconcern

Leadership Is...

Commitment

We all know the difference between contribution and commitment, which is well-illustrated in the story about the ham and egg breakfast: the chicken contributed, the pig was committed. I couldn't help think of that at my youngest granddaughter's first birthday recently, when she obviously fully committed to her cake.

Pat Miller, a dear friend and an accomplished leader from FedEx Express, was kind enough to relate this story to me; it helps identify, in part, what makes her tick, and is an excellent example of one reason leaders are successful - commitment.

Those who know Pat know she is a big fan of Soul Cycle - a New York City spinning studio that incorporates inspiration into a great workout, creating a total mind -body connection during each session. The studio is crowded and dark, candlelit only. The instructors are aggressive. They call you out by bike number if you slack off. But despite the environment, she always leaves class feeling relaxed, motivated and fit - often with inspiration she shares with her family, friends, and employees.

- Do we recognize the importance of life balance and the impact it can have on all aspects of your life, and do we take the necessary steps to ensure we capture it?

A few weeks ago, on the last hill in the class, the instructor chided her class for not pushing harder. *"Don't save your fearless!"* the instructor yelled as she came by each bike to see if they were really pushing themselves, "You can always find it again."

Don't save your fearless! What could that mean, and why did these words really hit home for Pat? She is a driver, always striving for improvement. These words resonated with her because she realized that until you test yourself, until you push to your limits, there is no fear, there is no ability to *show* your fearless.

- Do we become complacent and/or comfortable or do we stretch ourselves to reach our potential, in everything we do?
- Do we encourage others to do the same?

Don't save your fearless! How many times have you saved your fearless? Pat says she does it all the time. The idea she has that she doesn't bring up because others may think it is stupid. The excitement she has that she tones down so others think she is cool. The conversations she leaves thinking she shouldn't have said this or that. She often holds back, saving her fearless for the next meeting, the next call or the next conversation.

- Do we recognize the importance of continuous learning to the achievement of our potential and our goals?
- Do we see every interaction with someone and every assignment or challenge, as a learning opportunity to be embraced and not taken for granted?

During the recent recession, she was obsessed with articles about careers and professional development. She came across a headline listing the number one thing companies were looking for in employees. Slowly she worked her way through the article, anticipating the answer and her response. Would she have to enroll in another leadership class to stay competitive? Or would it be some other skill she lacked (hated) like statistics or something trendy like Six Sigma. The article talked about the number of companies surveyed and the high level of accuracy in the results. When she finally came to the answer, she was shocked. The number one thing everyone was looking for was creativity.

Creativity - how could that be? For years Pat had tried to hide hers, as do many of us. During her time in service in the Army, she felt they certainly did not appreciate creativity. Neither did Dell's manufacturing operation, where she had worked previously. As she researched the subject further, she discovered the world had changed. The old rules of "keep your head down" and "don't be noticed" became "stand up, speak up and be original and authentic." You might be judged, but that is better than being ignored.

- Do we limit our value by anticipating/guessing what others want rather than contributing all that we can?

Since then, she has tried to undo years of keeping her creativity under wraps. She tries new things and encourages her team to do the same. She embraces change and reads about new ideas weekly. But the other night, on the saddle in Soul Cycle, she realized that she was now just living in her creative comfort zone.

Now is the time to quit saving our fearless and really push our minds and spirits in the same way she pushed her body on the bike, to break through the nagging little fears that keep us from true innovation. We need to do what Pat does, to envision our bike number being called out by an aggressive spin master, for not pushing past our fear.

- Do we realize that every time we overcome 'our fearless,' we raise the bar of what we can do and accomplish?

She closed by telling me that every fiscal year she has a theme for herself and her team and this year's theme was going to be *Don't save your fearless.* She challenges us all to do this same, to rethink our objectives, our plans and to support and implement them in a bigger, bolder, fearless way.

- Do you truly understand yourself and who you are, what you stand for and the value you add?

If you do, you will not only be helping yourself, but you will be helping others as well. Don't save your fearless!

Commitment

Thoughts on commitment

- "Unless commitment is made, there are only promises ..." - *Peter F. Drucker*
- "Commitment turns a promise into reality with ... actions that speak louder than words." - *Steve Brunkhorst*
- "It is fatal to enter any war without the will to win it." - *General Douglas MacArthur*
- "You can't command commitment; you have to inspire it." – *James Kouzes and Barry Posner*

Ways leaders build commitment

- Announce and publish intentions and goals
- Have shared goals with the team
- Be involved and engaged
- Check the pulse of the organization regularly through 'skip level' meetings and surveys
- Clarify and reiterate values
- Personalize goals and objectives for each individual on the team; let them know their role and value, why it is important to them
- Establish a cause, not a plan
- Show commitment in everything you do, even to the smallest of details

Passion

[**pash**-*uh* n]:

...a strong enthusiasm, excitement, liking or desire for
or devotion to some activity, object, or concept

Synonyms: desire, urgency
Antonyms: indifference, apathy

Leadership Is...

Passion

The loud, shrill sound resonated down the long, dark hallway, shattering the silence of the night like the breaking of glass. We all stopped and stared at the telephone, knowing full well, as all parents do, that any call after the sun went down, could bring nothing but bad news.

Whom am I kidding?! We were in my freshman dorm at college; it was only about 9:30 pm; no one was sleeping; and no one had any clue at that time of what would later be the feeling of the dreaded late night call. There was, however, a long, dark corridor, dark because earlier that afternoon we had broken the light with an indoor soccer game. And, oh yes, there was a phone.

One of my dorm mates, Jim, answered the lone wall phone, probably hoping it was a girl. However, his first words dispelled any thought that it might have been a member of the opposite sex, "You're WHO?! From WHERE?! You're S#!%&ing me?" While the 24 boys who lived in this wing of the dorm may not have possessed many social skills, we all knew this was, as our mothers had so dutifully drilled into us, a huge social faux pax, and we began laughing.

Jim then turned around, and despite me standing in the hall only two doors away, yelled, "Bob, it's for you!" My smile quickly faded and, as I walked slowly to the phone, uncertainty and fearful thoughts were unleashed in my brain. But my thoughts did a 180 when I heard Jim scream, 'It's the F@*king Yankees!'

And indeed it was. Having been born and raised in New York, however, I have to admit getting a call from the legendary Yankees – Babe Ruth, Lou Gehrig, Mickey Mantle - it just didn't get any better than this! The call was, indeed, to ask me to play on one of their farm teams, but that is not what this story is all about.

- Do we provide our employees with those moments in life where they feel as if they are on top of the world – a moment they will never forget?

(Flashback 13 years.) For as long as I can remember, I loved baseball and wanted to be a ball player or manager or coach. The first Christmas present I can remember was not from my parents, but from someone I called Grandmamma Muchacha, who unfortunately, I can remember nothing about other than this present and that she would always give me Yoo Hoos, the chocolate drink endorsed by Yogi Berra from the drug store/mini-grocery under her apartment! But I will never forget the tiny plastic baseball glove, the small *real* wooden bat, and my first baseball, one of those soft ones made in Japan that when you actually hit it was permanently out of shape. She gave me these when I was 5 years old. I wore that glove and carried that ball everywhere.

When I was seven, I tried out for my first organized baseball team for 8 -12 year olds. I knew I was too young but had bugged my parents enough that they finally buckled and let me go. They did this because they knew how much it meant to me, despite their worries that my dreams would be crushed if I did not make it.

- Do we put aside our wishes to help others achieve their goals and potential?
- Do we push aside our prejudices and perceptions to give someone a chance?

I probably should have known they didn't think I would make it by the way they constantly told me don't get your hopes up, you're so much younger that the other boys, which, to those of us older and wiser, means you're not very good. Funny thing is, I admitted even then I wasn't very good, but I wasn't going to let that stop me from doing the thing I loved more than anything else in the world. I just knew I could do it! I had to!

I may be dating myself, but back in those days, getting to play on any organized team was not something everyone could do. You had to earn your spot on the roster or go home. And you did not get a trophy for just showing up. So when I arrived at tryouts, I was a scared little kid who, looking at my competition – almost a foot taller and bigger and stronger than I was - felt so-so about his ability to hit but very good about his speed and knowledge of the game. What I could not do, however - no matter how many times my parents, who were truly saints working with me every day in preparation for the big day - was catch a fly ball. They threw me thousands of pop flies, but I could not catch a one. I was lousy. They volunteered to buy me a new glove, hoping that would help, but we all knew that was not the problem.

- Do we look for excuses why things can't be done or do we find ways to make them a reality?

At tryouts, as luck would have it, catching fly balls was the last station I had to go to. I had been watching this area from the time I arrived, in anticipation and dread. The routine was the same, ten fly balls hit to you from a fungo bat. When one was dropped, the coaches would shake their heads as they looked down to write something on their clipboards and made comments to each other. After what seemed an eternity, my time finally came. As I ran to the outfield, heart beating much faster than it should even for a young boy, I noticed my parents, who eagerly and with encouragement had watched every other section of the tryout (batting, ground balls, running the bases), turn around so they would not have to watch my dream be shattered. I knew they loved me, but seeing them turn away, even if it was to save themselves the pain of seeing my dream broken, my heart filled with sadness, a sadness that quickly turned to doubt.

- Do we maintain high expectations for our employees and demonstrate a confidence in them?

I knew my limitations and my capabilities, but I was determined to succeed, so, when I heard the crack of the bat, and as the first fly ball was headed in my direction, my body trembling with fear and excitement, I put my glove heel against my lower chest, fingers pointing out and up toward the sky at a 45 degree angle and I ran to where I thought the downward trajectory of the ball would lead it. I got under it, knowing I was in the right position, and did what any other aspiring ball player with limited skills would do – I purposely let the ball hit me in the upper chest as I snapped the fingers of my glove tightly to my body, trapping the ball much like I envision the motion of a snap dragon capturing a fly that got too close to its leaves! And I caught it! One down, nine to go.

- Do we encourage and allow ingenuity and innovation in our quest for excellence, or are we locked into the ways of the past?

I followed this same routine for all ten of the fly balls that were hit to me that day, catching everyone but wincing more and louder with each successful catch. I went home that night optimistic – I did it! Not one fly ball hit the ground!

My parents, on the other hand, while proud of me, were concerned when they saw how sore, bruised and ugly my chest was! They took me to the doctor, who, after x-rays, told us he had never seen anything so badly bruised without anything broken, and made me promise to never do that again. Which I did - with my fingers crossed, just in case I made the team.

The next day I sat by the phone all day and was finally rewarded with a call that evening telling me I was going to be a Tiger! I was on cloud nine. As the year progressed it was obvious during practices and games that I was not – let's just say – the strongest player on the team, but my coach allowed me to participate probably because of my enthusiasm and desire.

- Do we give everyone a chance to participate and play a role in what we are trying to accomplish?

I had a record-setting first year, a 100% on base percentage. I got on base every time I got up to bat thanks to 28 walks in 28 at bats - during which I only swung the bat once. And I got to play right field; I was sure it was because I caught every fly ball during tryouts, but as I grew older, I realized that is where most teams put their worst player.

Needless to say, over the years I practiced hard, was blessed with supportive and loving parents, and had some wonderful, energetic, encouraging coaches to help me hone my skills so I could play the game I loved. I knew it was all worth it - that my dream could be fulfilled – when I received the call that night in 1968, in the freshman dorm in Ithaca, New York.

But somehow, looking back to that night, the call that was the most important, was the one 11 years earlier, not only because it gave me the chance to pursue my dream, but because it gave me the confidence to continue that pursuit by showing me I could do the impossible if I put my mind to it!

- Do we recognize the fire, the passion in ourselves and others?
- Do we fan the flames of that passion so we can all grow?

Passion

Thoughts on passion

- "A person can succeed at almost anything for which they have unlimited enthusiasm." – *Charles M. Schwab*
- "When you set yourself on fire, people love to come and see you burn." – *John Wesley*
- "A great leader's courage to fulfill his vision comes from passion, not position." – *John Maxwell*

Ways leaders ignite passion

- Allocate time at work for people to work on those things they enjoy
- Promote small groups or committees; allow some of these to be formed by employees based on their desires
- Facilitate group activities and events
- Make work enjoyable; relate individual passions to work related efforts
- Be active, involved and supportive
- Speak of and with your passion
- Talk of dreams and possibilities; 'paint a picture' of the future that can be
- Do something; act
- Reward beneficial behaviors
- Define and constantly reevaluate your passion

Receptivity

[ri-**sep**-ti- vi-tee]:

...willingness and capability to receive, especially, open and responsive to ideas, impressions, or suggestions

Synonyms: openness, approachability, interest
Antonyms: hostility, antagonism, enmity

Leadership Is...

Receptivity

Here is another story that you likely have heard before, but one that bears repeating. This version is one that a neighbor of mine shared with me shortly before moving out of town.

As an engineer, I recognize the value of establishing standards and metrics to help leaders drive a successful business, regardless of the industry they are in. One metric adopted by the U.S. Government and the U.S. Railroads was, and still is, the distance between the rails on train tracks: four feet, eight and a half inches (4' 8.5"). Go anywhere in the United States and you will find the distance between any two parallel rails, otherwise known as the railroad gauge, to be that width. I could understand the need for standardization - to keep the trains on the tracks wherever they should go - but I was curious as to why this odd, yet very specific distance, was chosen?

My initial quest for knowledge began with a discussion with my neighbor, who was involved in the railroad business, albeit in finance. When asked about this specific distance, his response was, "I am not sure, but *we have always done it that way*. So my journey began!"

Initial research uncovered that the U.S. Railroads were first built by English expatriates who adhered to the standards used for their tramways in their home. Tramways were the people-movers in England prior to railroads, and since the railroad workers were both familiar and satisfied with this standard, they adopted it as their own. While reasonable, it begs the question of why England set this as the standard for their tramways. When I inquired of a friend of British descent living here in Memphis, he responded, "I don't know, but *we have always done it that way.*"

The answer to why, however, was rather simple: the people who built the tramways, to save time and money, used the same jigs and tools used to build wagon wheels. So why, I then asked, were wagon wheels made with this precise spacing? The answer I got was (you guessed it): *we have always done it this way.* Further digging uncovered that distance was the optimum spacing to prevent wagons from breaking down when traveling throughout the countryside. And why were they breaking down? It was because any spacing other than this would not allow the wheels to fit in the wheel ruts already in those old and long-distance roads.

I concede that it may have been prudent to build the wheel base that distance to avoid damage, but for me it begged the question as to why those ruts were in the road in the first place

Looking into the history books, I found the roads throughout Europe were built by Imperial Rome to support their Legions. These same roads are still in use today. So how did the ruts get there? The initial ruts, the same ruts that everyone had to match for fear of damaging their wagons, were made by the

Roman chariots. These chariots were designed to very specific standards by the Roman Empire to provide greatest influence in ruling over their nation. They provided speed, stability and room to fight.

So now you know - the U.S. standard gauge of 4' 8.5" between railroad tracks is a result of the original military specifications set by ancient Rome for their army's chariots!

- Do we dig deep enough into issues to determine reasons or do we just take things for granted/on face value?

- Do we ask enough 'why' questions to get to the root cause?

However, one nagging question still remained for me. Why did Roman army war chariot wheels have such an odd sized spacing? I am sure one of the ancient Roman Generals would have told us, "Ego operor non vere teneo *have usquequaque perfectus is ut via*." (My best attempt at a translation of: I don't really know, but *we have always done it this way*.)

In reality, the Romans made this decision only after extensive research and experimentation; to maximize the speed and versatility, the chariots were designed to be pulled by two horses, not one. This very specific spacing (4' 8.5") represents the distance needed to accommodate the back end of two horses.

So the next time you are told, *we have always done it that way*, you might want to check to see if the rationale for current practices are based on fact and proven results - or if it just comes from the rear end of a horse!!

Receptivity

Thoughts on receptivity

- "People only see what they are prepared to see." - *Ralph Waldo Emerson*
- "Seeking means: to have a goal; but finding means to be free, to be receptive, to have no goal." - *Herman Hesse*
- "Let go of certainty. The opposite isn't uncertainty. It's openness, curiosity and a willingness to embrace paradox, rather than choose up sides... never stop trying to learn and grow." - *Tony Schwartz*

Ways leaders are receptive

- Have an 'open door policy'
- Are not judgmental
- Value input
- Ask questions
- Seek advice
- Share themselves
- Build on and merger ideas
- Read 'religiously'; practice continuous learning
- Read body language not just words
- Stay focused (e.g., eye contact)
- Continue thinking of ideas presented and respond after preliminary discussions

Teamwork

[**teem**-wurk]:

…work (efforts) done by several associates with each doing a part but all subordinating personal prominence to the efficiency of the whole

Synonyms: cooperation, collaboration
Antonyms: selfishness, independence

Leadership Is...

Teamwork

Are you a country or city boy/girl? Me, I am an original New Yorker, from near The Big Apple no less. And while I did not take advantage of it the way many do, the city is a great place to live: Broadway shows, professional sports of all kinds, museums, subways, shopping, great restaurants, and much more.

Maybe it is because I am from the city that I find small towns a real treat to visit. They are usually very quiet, often in a very picturesque area of the country, with people who know everyone else, who can spot a stranger coming but still treat them as family.

As I was reading the paper a few months ago while traveling in Missouri, I was reminded that there is one thing that both city and country people have in common – they are proud of their local communities and who they are. The front page article that day was about how everyone was getting ready for the wheel-barrow races, the food festivals, the greased pig contest, and of course, the rides. You guessed it; they were preparing for their County Fair! And while I have not been to many, I would have to say that there is nothing like a small County Fair.

My older daughter went to school in St. Louis, and it was near there, just before the annual horse auction began as part of a Missouri county fair, the farmers gathered for a wagon-pull to show off their largest and strongest Clydesdales. One year, two farmers each had a horse, the likes of which had not been seen in that area for quite some time. The whole county was abuzz with anticipation (and a little local bragging) of what was to be a spectacular event billed as a competition between 'the biggest and best.'

And they were not disappointed! As the competition began, both horses pulled with all their might. Both easily passed the previous record of 27,000 pounds set three years ago during this same event. They kept pulling and finally, with sweat running off both animals, one was declared the winner at 28,800 pounds.

After a short while, the owners thought it might be interesting to pair up these two horses and see what they could do together. The crowd was curious to see if, even while tired from the competition, they could beat the combined weight of their last pulls - 57,800 pounds. So they hitched them together to the sled. To everyone's surprise, they quickly passed the 57,800 pound mark; then to the amazement of the crowd, they continued pulling together until they pulled a load of over 86,000 pounds, almost 30,000 pounds more than their combined pulls!

- Do we recognize the value of true teamwork?

- Do we allow, encourage and set up opportunities for people to work together as a team?

- Do we maximize performance through encouragement and the environment we create?

Leaders know the sum *must* be greater than the sum of its parts, and prepares an environment that makes it possible.

Teamwork

Thoughts on teamwork

- "When a team outgrows individual performance and learns team confidence, excellence becomes a reality." - *Joe Paterno*
- "A group becomes a team when each member is sure enough of himself and his contribution to praise the skills of the others." - *Norman Shidle*
- "Cooperation is the thorough conviction that nobody can get there unless everybody gets there." - *Virginia Burden*

Ways leaders foster teamwork

- Create diverse teams; select the right 'mix' of employees
- Set clear team mission and vision
- Define roles and responsibilities of all
- Play to individuals' strengths
- Coach and participate themselves
- Be available as needed
- Celebrate small wins and sought after behaviors
- Delegate and empower
- Practice, practice, practice (together)
- Hold frequent group meetings
- Ensure everyone participates and speaks freely
- Make teamwork part of performance criteria

Putting It All Together

[poo t eng it awl t*uh*-**geth** -er]:

...a collection of related items; *especially* one to be considered or acted on together

Synonyms: putting together, pervasive
Antonyms: disassembly, destruction

Leadership Is...

Putting It All Together

All I wanted was to fix up my new old house! I am sure many of you have had the same experience. I became a first time home owner back in 1979, when I purchased an older home in the Memphis area. Since it occurred early in my career, there were limited funds, but being the eternal optimist, I just knew that I could fix it up despite protests from my wife who knows that I am inept in self-help. Even I must admit, if it cannot be repaired with a hammer or superglue, as far as I am concerned, it cannot be repaired!

Looking back, I realize that I learned a lot about leadership skills during this adventure. Step one was easy. Gayle and I decided on a vision for how we wanted our new home to look and prioritized the work. When most items turned out to be top priority, and because the timeline to get them done was too far into the future, we decided to make it more manageable. We broke the initiatives into specific tasks, identifying and buying the tools required to accomplish them.

- Do we always define our goals and objectives?

- Do we prioritize our objectives and actions to remain focused?

- Do we recognize the value of project planning/project management to ensure timeliness and quality goals were met?

Our next step was to define the resources required to get this all done within a weekend. The compilation of our hoped for all-volunteer team began. We thought that this would not be too difficult, for between Church, work, soccer, school and neighbors, surely we would be able to get the help needed.

- Do we take advantage of our networks to facilitate improvements and procure the right support?

So we explained our vision to everyone we knew, knowing that they would be overcome by our passion. We were so excited, and knew they would be too, that we even wondered how we would tell all those late-comers wishing to help that there were no more tasks for them to do. Much to our surprise, however, a week before our 'work day,' we only had 2 volunteers, and they were both members of our family who were obligated to help. It was obviously time for Plan B.

- Do we understand the value of contingency planning?

Our Plan B consisted of offering bribes - I mean encouragements - for those who came to help. The biggest surge in volunteers occurred when we offered free beer for all. As a result, we raised the number on our team to 14, a number that would work for our overall project plan.

- Do we use incentives effectively?

The day finally came for the work to be done. My wife, always the pragmatist, came up with the idea to fill our washing machine with ice and fill it with the beer. It held a lot, would keep the drinks cold and we just had to turn on the washer to get rid of the melted ice. Brilliant!

- Do we employ and encourage creativity and innovation in programs and efforts?

When all were gathered (amazingly, they all showed up), we held a pre-work meeting, at which we divided the group into teams; we assigned ourselves to teams as well, delegated the work among the teams and reiterated our goals for the day, all those necessary steps to successful project management. We were proud of ourselves and very optimistic!

- Do we provide a clear vision for the team and let everyone know the role and value they provide?
- Do we ensure detailed communication of roles and responsibilities, and allow others to participate in assignments and to ask questions as necessary?

Gayle's team was responsible for the lawn and garden. It wasn't long, however, before she was called into the house to help with a kitchen related incident. It seems the person assigned to clean up the kitchen thought their role included cleaning out the refrigerator, and proceeded to dump a large pot of freshly made French onion soup down the disposal because 'it smelled bad.' We could have lived with that had it not been for the friend who was under the house, more specifically under the sink drain, replacing a pipe. He did not seem to think it was funny when we all snickered when we saw him drenched and covered in soggy onions. One down, thirteen to go!

- Do we make sure everyone knows how their piece fits with the overall game plan or do we only give people specific tasks to perform without the big picture?

- Are we flexible enough to move resources around according as the need arises?

I assigned myself to the more difficult chore of painting the outside of the house. I took the assignment of painting the top portion of the house myself and asked the others to do the first level.

- Again, do we recognize the power of leading by example?

After a few hours of painting, while hanging upside down trying to paint the corners of the eaves, I hollered down to the others to see how they were progressing. The silence was deafening! Worried, I climbed down and not finding anyone outside (they couldn't all have gone to the bathroom at the same time, could they?) I went in and found them in the laundry room, each with a can of beer in his hand. And based on how loud each was speaking and the constant laughter, I could tell they had been there for some time.

- Do we regularly monitor progress against agreed upon milestones and sufficient time during the project to communicate with others allow others?

- Do we understand the difference between incentive and reward?

When the day was over, Gayle and I stood out front and stared at our home. Our gaze was focused on the muted yellow color we had chosen for the outside of the house, which started at the brown eaves and window trim – both of which I painted - and ending in what appeared to be a graph of a company's profit chart. Our friends had merely stopped painting at - and wound up outlining - the trees, shrubs and plants in our front flower bed. In retrospect it may have been a bad idea to ask the painting team to return to work after I found them inside, although I have to admit, at the time they seemed to be willing to try anything that was asked of them.

- Do we make the tough decisions 'under fire' for expediency or do we enforce the quality, timing and quantity objectives we established initially?

Gayle and I did the only thing we could at the time. We went inside, sat at the dining room table, opened a bottle of wine, poured ourselves a glass, and talked and laughed about the day and the lessons learned.

- Do we take responsibility for the actions and results of our team?
- Do we conduct 'after action reviews' to recognize and celebrate the successes and to learn how things can be improved going forward?

As we sat there together we were both reminded of a quote by Thomas A. Edison: "I learn more from my failures than I do from my successes." Oh, how true!

Putting It All Together

Thoughts on putting it all together

- "Life is a puzzle. Putting it together is the challenge." – *Anonymous*
- "Holism traditionally says that a collection ... may have a collective property that cannot be inferred from the properties of its members." - *C. West Churchman*
- "The whole is greater than the sum of its parts." – *Aristotle*

Ways leaders put it all together

- Stay focused
- Remain true to self
- Do what is right, not what is easy or convenient
- Tend to 'the little things'
- Seek, assimilate and use feedback from others
- Attend to the good of the 'whole'
- Maintain life balance
- Eliminate behavioral and value boundaries between work and personal
- Trust others
- Trust self
- Review self regularly
- Care
- 'Play on' strengths

Acknowledgements

(pictures)

1. **Culture** - Gayle Bennett, bennettgb@aol.com
2. **Problem Solving** – Gayle Bennett, bennettgb@aol.com
3. **Humility** – clker.com free clip art,
   http://www.clipartbest.com/clipart-KTnekL7Gc
4. **Ethics** – HistoryLink101, http://historylink101.com/ww2-planes/aa-b-17-bomber.htm
5. **Customer Fanatic** - Wikipedia,
   http://en.wikipedia.org/wiki/File:Vasnetsov_Grave_digger.JPG
6. **Diversity** - Delicious Dishings, http://megan-deliciousdishings.blogspot.com/2009_10_01_archive.html
7. **Preparation** – Mononews Blog, photo credit to
   tcatcarson@yahoo.co.uk
   http://blog.mononews.ca/2012/06/all-the-worlds-a-stage/
8. **Appreciation** – Alphabet Soup,
   http://julestorti.wordpress.com/2011/10/27/can-we-parent-proof-our-travels/
9. **Focus** – Gayle Bennett, bennettgb@aol.com
10. **Courage** - Gayle Bennett, bennettgb@aol.com
11. **Communication** – Widescreen Wallpapers, http://wide-wallpapers.net/st-patricks-cathedral-new-york-city-wide-wallpaper/
12. **Facilitation** – Gayle Bennett, bennettgb@aol.com

Acknowledgements

(pictures)

13. **Networking** – Susan Puckett, http://susan-puckett.squarespace.com/my-blog/2013/5/22/what-ive-been-missing-in-water-valley
14. **Feedback** – BeautySophia, http://beautysophia.com/home-3/
15. **Adaptability** – Wikipedia, http://en.wikipedia.org/wiki/File:Rafting_em_Brotas.jpg
16. **Perseverance** – Widescreen Wallpapers, http://wide-wallpapers.net/us-flag-2-wide-wallpaper/
17. **Vision** - Planet Houston AMX, http://www.planethoustonamx.com/stuff/continental-airlines-gremlin.htm
18. **Positive Expectations** – XarJ Blog and Podcast, http://www.xarj.net/2008/cat-painting/
19. **Prioritization** – 4 Free Photos, www.4freephotos.com
20. **Trust** – Gayle Bennett, bennettgb@aol.com
21. **Respect** – Gayle Bennett, bennettgb@aol.com http://www.commercialappeal.com/photos/2011/jul/17/233185/
22. **Reputation** – Animal Photos, http://animalphotos.org/german-shepherd-2-3964
23. **Integrity** - Answers, http://dogs.answers.com/caring-for-dogs/know-how-to-bury-your-dog-in-your-backyard-safely

Acknowledgements

(pictures)

24. **Utilization** – In a Mirror Dimly, http://inamirrordimly.net/2010/06/of-cracked-pots-and-final-preparations/
25. **Responsibility** – Gayle Bennett, bennettgb@aol.com
26. **Compassion** –The Salvation Army, http://www.be-an-angel.org.uk/changinglives
27. **Commitment** – Gayle Bennett, bennettgb@aol.com
28. **Passion** – HD Nice Wallpapers, http://www.hdnicewallpapers.com/Wallpaper-Download/Baseball/Baseball-Ball-Bat-and-Glove
29. **Receptivity** – clker.com free clip art, http://www.clker.com/clipart-64815.html
30. **Teamwork** - Northern Development, http://www.northerndevelopment.bc.ca/explore-our-region/success-stories/lakes-district-fall-fair-undergoes-a-whirlwind-renovation/
31. **Putting It All Together** – SandandSisal, http://sandandsisal.com/2014/03/dont-cry-over-spilled-paint.html

About The Author

As Chief Learning Officer of the world's largest express transportation company, Bob Bennett understands the imperative role employees and leaders play in the strategic success of a company. Prior to his retirement, his scope of responsibilities included defining the role of Human Resources for FedEx Express and providing strategic and tactical direction for the development and execution of programs for the continuous learning and growth of its more than 150,000 employees in more than 220 countries and territories world-wide.

With a background in engineering and extensive experience in global operations, Bob has a real world perspective and deep respect for the effect that employees and corporate culture have on a company's bottom line and the responsibilities of management in this process. Under his leadership, FedEx continued to nurture a culture founded on People-Service-Profit. Simply stated, it is the belief that if you take care of your people, they will provide outstanding service and profits will follow. He has carried this passion for leadership and culture to his new position as Founder of Achieve-LLC, a company dedicated to leadership development and organizational effectiveness.

Through Bob's guidance, FedEx Express created even stronger employee focus through employee loyalty surveys, prescriptive coaching, market-based management programs and enhanced learning performance metrics. During his tenure, FedEx consistently ranked on Fortunate Magazine's list of the "World's Most Admired Companies' and was ranked 5th on the Great Place to Work Institute's 2011 list of the World's Best Multinational Workplaces.

A passionate advocate for expanding the role of HR from "bricklayer to architect," especially in the area of leadership development, Bob was instrumental in establishing the FedEx talent management program to assess high performance and high potential employees. He also led a progressive initiative to integrate strategic workforce planning into employee development, talent management, talent review, performance management and succession planning. In effect, the initiative created a clear roadmap for achieving business success through human capital management.

A native New Yorker, Bob earned bachelor's and master's degrees in Industrial Engineering from Cornell University and a master's degree in business administration from Bernard Baruch College at the City University of New York. He is a sought after speaker whose portfolio includes The Economist Talent Summit, The Milken Institute Global Conference, Human Capital Institute Symposium, CLO Summit, Corporate Learning Week, as well as featured articles in CLO Magazine and Oxford Economics. Bob serves on many community boards, including The Salvation Army.

Bob believes in learning from each other, and welcomes your stories, comments and feedback at <u>bob@achieve-llc.com</u> or on Twitter at @bob_achieve.